The Cry at Salem: America's Witchcraft Trials

BY JEFFREY JON RICHARDS

WIPF & STOCK · Eugene, Oregon

WIPF AND STOCK PUBLISHERS
199 W 8th Avenue, Suite 3
Eugene OR 97401

http://www.wipfandstock.com

THE CRY AT SALEM:
America's Witchcraft Trials

By Jeffrey Jon Richards

Copyright © 2002 by Jeffrey Jon Richards

ISBN: 978-1-59244-103-7

The Cry at Salem:
America's Witchcraft Trials

TABLE OF CONTENTS

PREFACE 3
INTRODUCTION..5

CHAPTER I:
THE CAUSES FOR THE BELIEF IN THE PREVALENCE OF WITCHES IN SALEM VILLAGE
The Puritan Concept of Being Chosen and Its Impact 11
Religious Problems..15
Political Problems..19
Fear of Indians 21
Social Problems 23

CHAPTER II:
A BACKGROUND OF THE ACCUSERS AND THE ACCUSED
The Accusers 27
The Accused 32
Accusations: Justified or Biased 43

CHAPTER III:
STATISTICS AND TRAITS OF INDIVIDUALS INVOLVED WITH THE SALEM WITCH TRIALSS
Statistics 47
Traits 51

CHAPTER IV:
THE TRIAL SYSTEM OF THE SALEM WITCH TRIALS
The Court of Oyer and Terminer..57
The Role of the Clergy and Judges 59
Confession 61
Spectral Evidence 62
Results of the Trials 64

CONCLUSION 67
NOTES ON CHAPTERS 71
SELECTED BIBLIOGRAPHY 89
ABOUT THE AUTHOR 105

THE CRY AT SALEM: AMERICA'S WITCHCRAFT TRIALS

Preface

Remembering the Salem Witch Trials recalls events of a major historical episode in American history. After three hundred years many will discover, or rediscover, what occurred in Salem village about three hundred years ago. Perhaps the burning question surrounding the trials is "Why did this happen?" To that persistent question there have been a host of solutions offered, ranging from Satanic intervention to mental derangement caused by a fungus indigenous to the area.

The writer does not claim to be the final word on the subject. For in attempting to unravel the mysteries of exactly what took place, we are in a sense left to speculation. The Salem Witch Trials are a puzzle. However, I believe there have been left for us today enough pieces to reconstruct a reasonably accurate picture of what transpired in that volatile courtroom in the seventeenth century.

As one reads the accounts, one must remember the mindset of the period; we cannot judge the participants by our standards of the twenty-first century. However, with all of our sophistication, we could ask if human nature has changed in the past three hundred years. In this new millennium and century alone, we have witnessed horrible atrocities humans have inflicted upon each other — some so repulsive as to make the witch trials seem somewhat trivial.

Perhaps the spirit of the Salem Witch Trials is viable today in another form. In remembering the Salem Witch Trials there must not only be an awareness of this historical event, but also a determination that the spirit of the trials, whatever form it could take, will not be part of contemporary or future American life.

Jeffrey J. Richards
Salisbury, NC
Winter 2003

INTRODUCTION

It is very difficult for one to uncover and speculate what forces led to a world renown event. The student of history must not give priority to a single immediate cause but must keep in mind no such cause adequately explains a historical episode. In order to explain the Salem Witch Trials it must be realized that they occurred because of a culmination and synthesis of many covert and overt factors. One cannot say that it was only out of fear of witches, but rather, there were a myriad of reasons which led to the tragic event.

Western Europe had several decades prior to the seventeenth century experienced witchcraft mania. It spread from Rome to Bremen and Scotland. Bishop Jewell delivered a sermon on witchcraft before Queen Elizabeth in 1562. Baxter in his work, *Certainty of the World of Spirits*, confirmed in the minds of many the reality and formidable power of the unseen world.[1] Witchcraft, then, was not peculiar to Massachusetts, but was common to all of Europe. Louis of Palamo, an inquisitor of Sicily who sent many to death by burning, estimated that thirty thousand had been executed for witchcraft between 1450 and 1597.[2] Starkey claims a more accurate figure is hundreds of thousands.[3] Elizabeth Bacon claims that 200,000 to 300,000 is correct.[4] The belief in witchcraft seemingly has been with humankind throughout its history. Nugent writes:

5

THE CRY AT SALEM: AMERICA'S WITCHCRAFT TRIALS

Witchcraft itself is better characterized than defined, for it has varying creedal, liturgical, psychical, magical, moral and historical dimensions. Viewed broadly, it is more than a "Christian heresy" for it is older than and can be found independently of Christianity. Western witches sometimes call it "the old religion," a primitive pre-Christian religion with druidic and classic associations. It is an open question whether it is rooted in Hecate, Diana, Dionysus, Cain, Satan or resources of the psyche itself.[5]

Warren claims witchcraft has its source in the Greco-Roman world.[6]

This book is concerned primarily with the Puritans and their preoccupation with witchcraft. Even within Puritanism in the sixteenth century and over a hundred years before the Salem Witch Trials, there was much literature written on this subject which influenced many profoundly.

George Gifford, the Puritan minister of Maldon in Essex, also contributed two discussions in <u>a discourse of the subtill practices of devilles by witches and sorcerers</u> (1587) and <u>a dialogue concerning witches and witchcraftes</u> (1593). Finally, the controversy was brought to Scotland when James VI published his *Daemonologie* in Edinburgh in 1597.[7]

The colonists had emigrated from England to Plymouth in 1620. Only a decade before this date ten individuals were accused as witches in the Lancaster trial; all ten met their deaths at the gallows.[8] It is obvious that the Puritans were concerned with the subject of witchcraft and

INTRODUCTION

that it had a prominent place in their thinking. This was especially true after their exodus from England and to the colonies. Fisk claims:

> Their exodus was that of a chosen people who were at length to lay the everlasting foundations of God's kingdom upon earth.... In every propitious event they saw a special providence, an act of divine intervention to deliver them from the snares of an ever watchful Satan.[9]

Thus, the temperament and climate were conducive for belief in the prevalence of witches in the colonies. They had experienced it in their mother country, and since they were God's chosen, they should expect nothing different in the colonies.

The need for this work is related to the preliminary remarks. It has been displayed that the belief in witchcraft was prevalent in Europe before the Puritans came to the colonies and that many were executed for practicing it. However, there are a myriad of interpretations of what caused the outbreak of witchcraft in the colonies. One cannot logically state that a direct comparison can be made between colonial and European witchcraft. It is true that there are many similarities, but there are also many differences. The Puritans found themselves in a strange and foreign land, and the colonial environment was not as sophisticated as mother country and mainland Europe. The witchcraft in Europe was not peculiar to any one religious group, while our study is concerned with only the Puritans. Also, the majority of witchcraft executions in Europe occurred in a different historical context. The colonists seemingly had a precedent upon which to build since the fifteenth and sixteenth centuries witnessed many executions.

The Cry at Salem: America's Witchcraft Trials

One must endeavor to understand the historical context and not view the trials as an isolated event. There were many factors involved within the latter part of the seventeenth century which contributed to an air of witchcraft expectancy, and it is not valid to claim that one factor alone was responsible. Contemporaries saw the causes as totally Satanic. Cotton Mather writes:

> The New-Englanders are a People of God settled in those, which were once the Devil's Territories; and it may easily be supposed that the Devil was exceedingly disturbed, when he perceived such a People here accomplishing the Promise of old made unto our Blessed Jesus. That He should have the Utmost parts of the Earth for his Possession.... We have been advised by some Credible Christians yet alive, that a malefactor, accused of Witchcraft ... and Executed in this place more than Forty Years ago did then give Notice of, An Horrible Plot against the Country by Witchcraft.... And we have now with Horror seen the Discovery of such a Witchcraft![10]

However, others have attempted to explain the causes in more concrete terms. Corporael believes the symptoms of those who claimed they had been bewitched in Salem were caused by a fungus called ergot. She claims the symptoms alluded to in the Salem witchcraft records match those of ergot poisoning.[11] Perhaps the answer to the causes for the prevailing belief in witchcraft is found somewhere between a totally rationalistic and spiritual view.

Within the period of trials, one is able to clearly see that Puritanism in colonial Massachusetts was replete with social, political, psychological,

INTRODUCTION

and religious problems. There is a need to attempt to uncover the causes for the Salem Witch Trials. Such an analysis will enable one to understand not only this isolated event in 1692 but also the latter part of seventeenth century colonial America. Specifically one should come to a better understanding of the reasons for the Puritan demise in the colonies. The Puritans, of course, desired to build a covenant community. However, through a series of setbacks and problems culminating in the witchcraft trials, the ideal for such a spiritual paradise was lost. The decline of the Puritan dream was initiated by a series of sixteenth century events which included the Half-Way Covenant, Stoddardeanism, and finally the Salem Witch Trials. Drake succinctly states concerning the importance of the Salem Witch Trials:

> Salem has thus become the focal point of historical analysis of colonial witchcraft. The outburst of 1692 has been effectively separated from its American ancestry, and its origins located somewhere in the 1680s. Earlier cases have been ignored and miscounted. For there were over 95 incidents involving colonial people with witchcraft before 1692.[12]

The primary purpose is to attempt to display that two causes for the Salem Witch Trials were various social and psychological factors prevalent within Salem Village and surrounding communities. A second intention is to view the actual trials and the various methods of judicial proceedings. A third goal of this book is to attempt to give a broad view of the historical context and how this one event fits into the flow of colonial history of the latter years of seventeenth century Massachusetts.

The Salem Witch Trials occurred over three hundred years ago; thus, the majority of our sources will be secondary. There are, however, several secondary works which are excellent. Some of the are Jones's *The Shattered Synthesis,* Erikson's *Wayward Puritans,* Ellis's *The Puritan Age and Rule in Massachusetts,* Murdock's *Literature and Theology in Colonial New England,* and Starkey's *The Devil in Massachusetts.* There are a number of excellent primary sources, and some of them record the actual trial proceedings. These include the following: Drake's *Annals of Witchcraft in New England* and *The Witchcraft Delusion in New England,* Mather's *Boniface: An Essay to Do Good, The Diary of Cotton Mather,* and Upham's *Salem Witchcraft.* Even though such sources are at one's disposal, it is tempting to form a conclusion by personal opinions and biases. This book will attempt to weigh evidences and form valid and objective conclusions.

There are some obvious limitations of a study of the Salem Witch Trials. First, there are more than three hundred years between the present and the date of this event. Second, the primary sources are written by men who reflect the thinking and intellectual climate of their times. The clergy were the interpreters of the witchcraft phenomenon, and, of course, their interpretations were primarily spiritual. Third, even though there were many historical forces crescendoing and culminating in the event of the Salem Witch Trials, it is possible only to view those which were major.

CHAPTER 1

THE CAUSES FOR THE BELIEF IN THE PREVALENCE OF WITCHES IN SALEM VILLAGE

THE PURITAN CONCEPT OF BEING CHOSEN OF GOD AND ITS IMPACT

The colony of Massachusetts Bay was an outgrowth of a fishing port developed in 1623 at Cape Ann. However, this site was not well suited for either fishing or farming, and the Dorchester promoters withdrew their financial support and returned to England in 1626. There remained only a small number, thirty or more, and they moved south to Naumkeag or Salem as it would be called.[1] They believed their mission was to extend the Gospel. Edward Johnson wrote in his diary: "At their arrivall those small number of Christians gathered at Salem, greatly rejoycing and the more, because they saw so many that came chiefly for promoting the great work of Christ in hand."[2] The settlers of Salem were Puritans, and they brought with them a strong Calvinistic theology and philosophy. However, Miller claims their theology was a modified Calvinism. He states: "The New Englanders did not stem directly from Calvin; they learned the

The Cry at Salem: America's Witchcraft Trials

Calvinistic theology only after it had been improved, embellished, and in many respects transformed by a host of hard-thinking expounders and critics."[3]

Prominent in their thinking was the concept that they were in a covenant relationship with God.

> Both in the works of all these men including Cotton, Hooker ... and in their lives is evidence for asserting that they constituted a particular school, that they worked out a special and peculiar version of theology which has a marked individuality which differentiates them considerably from followers of unadulterated Calvinism. And the central concept in their thought is the elaborate doctrine of the covenant.[4]

A covenant relationship with God was seen to exist when a set group bound themselves together in agreement to be obedient to God and seek the best for his neighbor.[5] Each particular congregation who bound themselves to such an agreement claimed Scripture for their authority. They saw themselves under the same covenant as was Israel. This covenant relationship gave each local congregation a sense of independence as each was not responsible to bishops or assemblies but to God alone.[6] They saw themselves as a chosen group set aside for a special task.

> They were convinced of the dire need for godly politics and determined to let God's infallible word guide their endeavors.... Their goal was to see the kingdom of Jesus Christ come to expression in society as well as the private, inner heart of man.[7]

THE CAUSES FOR THE BELIEF

What effects did the concept of the covenant relationship have upon the settlers at Salem? Primarily, they were convinced that they were to construct a model of Israel in the new world.[8] There was a strong sense of destiny in their thinking, and they as His elect had a vital mission to assume. However, there was an ever-pervading dread of failure and susceptibility to the whims of Satan. Since they were God's chosen, they reasoned, Satan and his forces would continually strive to subvert their mission. The feeling that they were on unholy ground was prominent in their thinking. "And haunting many ... was the knowledge that New England was not inherently holy, that it too could be relegated to the historical ash heap of places which no longer served the purposes of an electing God."[9]

Since the Puritans believed that they were in a covenant relationship with God, they expected there would be many battles with opposing forces. This had been the situation with Israel; therefore, why should their experience be different. This analogy impressed upon the mind of the Puritan caused him to see his enemy, primarily his archenemy Satan, even in the chaotic conditions resulting from nature herself. The Puritans viewed the unregenerate person's will as corrupt and dominated by self love and Satan.[10] Since the Half-Way Covenant made it possible for unregenerate people to be church members, the Puritans were aware that there were some among them who were of the kingdom of darkness rather than light. This caused them to view their enemy not only from without but also from within. The history of Israel was replete with personal failure; they sinned grossly against the Lord repeatedly. As Israel failed because of spiritual declension, the Puritans believed the same could happen to them. Foster writes:

THE CRY AT SALEM: AMERICA'S WITCHCRAFT TRIALS

In a real sense New England was founded so that it might decline. From the first it was to be a new Israel, and the story of the twelve tribes, new and old, would be incomplete without a concluding tale of the falling away from God, of the wrath of Jehovah, of temporary revivals, and finally of ultimate failure.[11]

An expression of this failure was a trend toward secularism. Many felt that to say the Puritans were becoming American was to confess their mission had failed. Many began wearing elaborate English clothes and long hair. "These apostasies were so diligently damned by the ministers that by the close of the seventeenth century, an enormous mass of clerical agony had accumulated, signifying a crisis in the Puritan soul."[12] Much of the preaching concerning Satan and his tactics was aimed at the younger people. Cotton Mather was certain that one of Satan's motives was to enslave them. They were firmly convinced that since they were God's covenant people, Satan and his diabolical forces would do anything to make their mission fail. It was because of this great fear that Mather especially exhorted young people to beware of Satan's tactics.

> To appeal to the imaginations of the young, Mather portrayed Satan as an old man whose special interest was to capture and enslave young people.... With this renewed emphasis upon the figure of Satan in the colonies in the late 1680s, it is not surprising that the witchcraft episode occurred during the brief period of confusion and doubt.[13]

The Puritans believed Satan used various individuals to effect his work in their domain. The Puritans also believed that Satan personally existed among them, and many claimed to have personally seen him. "The

THE CAUSES FOR THE BELIEF

number of people who had seen him [Satan], and who agreed with this description was large. To deny him was to deny God. And since he must have agents to work his will upon the earth, it were [*sic*] folly to deny witches."[14]

Religious Problems

There were certain religious problems from without and within Puritanism that bred an atmosphere of tension and anxiety. The Puritans were constantly threatened by Anglicanism. The first settlers of Salem decided that they would not be dependent upon their mother church but rather sought to be independent of her. At Salem in 1628 the Puritans broke with the principles of the Episcopal mother church. A simple covenant was adopted, and instead of gaining acceptance by the Church of England, they were ordained by the laying on of hands.[15]

The primary difference between the Puritans and the Church of England was that the former confined baptism to believers and their children. Only adults were to be admitted to full membership in the Church of England, and this could be done only after signing the covenant and the act of public confession.[16]

The misunderstanding between Anglicanism and Puritanism had begun before the 1690s; Roger Williams did much to promote great misunderstanding between the two groups. "Roger Williams had arrived in New England and had engaged in trade with the Indians. At Salem in 1633 and 1634 he began teaching that the churches in England were no true churches."[17] However, the problem came to its climax under the leadership of the royal governor, Edmund Andros, in the late 1680s. Andros was given instructions to encourage Anglicanism in Massachusetts. However, in carrying out royal instructions, he displayed a great lack of knowledge for the Puritan temperament. Andros requested the use of the meeting house, but Increase Mather and other ministers refused. The governor, therefore, by force took control of the Third Church and held Anglican Services there.[18] Soon after this event Andros was removed; the attempt to establish Anglicanism had failed. The threat of Anglicanism, however, had a profound influence upon the Puritans in Massachusetts Bay. They viewed Anglicanism as a compromise between their own Calvinistic doctrine and the Church of Rome which they detested.[19] They were God's chosen and covenant people, and the Church of England had threatened them.

However, there were also religious problems within the ranks of Puritanism. Perhaps one of the major problems stemmed back to the Half-Way Covenant and Stoddardeanism; both provided church membership to be based upon a social relationship and birth inheritance. The Puritans, though, considered everyone as a potential saint.[20] The need for a personal decision became secondary; a sectarian spirit became prominent within the Puritan ranks.[21] During the latter years of the seventeenth century, the ministers sensing the spiritual decline began to preach sermons designed to thwart the secular spirit. Many of the sermons of the period were full of harsh prophecies concerning the future of Massachusetts Bay and New England in general.[22]

> In the eyes of the Puritan clergy, the latter decades of the century were a troubled time for the colony of Massachusetts Bay. Perry

THE CAUSES FOR THE BELIEF

Miller has demonstrated very well the anxiety of the ministers and their increasing reliance upon the jeremiad to steer the straying colonists onto God's path.... According to the clergy, the great danger — and the cause for divine displeasure — was increasing secularization in the life of the colony and the consequent loss of religious zeal.[23]

Divine punishment was promised if they did not reform their ways.[24] However, a great deal of the preaching did not meet the needs of the average individual. It was of high intellectual character usually concerned with statements of abstruse theological dogma.[25] There were two extremes of preaching, the sermon which instilled fear and the sermon which because of its high intellectual quality did not meet the people's needs. What were the consequences of these two types of sermons? The former caused the individual to be introspective and apprehensive concerning his personal relationship with God. Many historians claim there was a spirit of doubt and fear in the churches in the late 1680s and 1690s.[26] The latter left a vacuum in the individual's soul, thus possibly resulting in melancholy. While one indeed has to carefully weigh Puritan skeptics who claim that they were characterized by melancholy, there may be some validity to the charge.[27] There was, at least, a climate which could produce such a state.

In 1689 Samuel Parris was called as pastor to Salem Village. However, he did not enjoy the respect that was usually common to Puritan ministers in New England; many openly opposed him. He was a Harvard dropout as he relinquished his studies to become a merchant in the West Indies. The people in Salem had a history of being discontent with their ministers; the two which were there before Parris left in quick succession since they were agitated with the situation in Salem. The atmosphere was tense and the situation was such that there would be great discontent with Parris.[28] Samuel Parris's presence in Salem caused great dissension and produced a factious spirit. To make matters worse, the basis for his salary was by a system of voluntary contributions.[29]

> Matters were made worse by Parris's course and arrogant manners, and his excessive severity in afflicting church discipline for trivial offenses. By 1691 the factions into which the village was divided were ready to fly at each other's throats.[30]

The situation, then, in Salem was potentially explosive for at the heart of their settlement there were serious problems.

While a trader in the West Indies, Samuel Parris acquired two slaves, both of whom he brought to Salem. He had a nine-year-old daughter, Betty, and an eleven-year-old niece named Abigale Williams. These two girls were highly emotional, and Betty, the younger of the two, would readily follow and obey all suggestions of Abigale.[31] Abigale preferred more exciting activities, anything that would take her away from the routine life that Salem offered. Her Puritan culture frowned upon frivolous amusements even for children.[32] Soon Tituba, one of Samuel Parris's slaves, had captivated the two children and several of their friends. She would read their palms and tell them the occupations of their future husbands. Hale claims she endeavored to perform the latter through the egg and glass method. "The egg and glass is an English folk method of divining. The white of an egg is poured into a glass and the subject stares into the egg white.... It is a method, in short, for producing an hallucination."[33]

THE CAUSES FOR THE BELIEF

Even though Hales's theory is possible, there is no documented proof for it. All agree that Tituba ignited their fears by her secret magic performances for the children. Many of the girls were thrilled with Tituba and her antics, especially Abigale. The Puritans believed that anything connected with witchcraft was associated with Satan. The girls knew this, but Tituba had a strong and peculiar control over them. The covert meetings at Reverend Parris's house were a manifestation of many unnoticeable factors in this community. It is true that the séances with Tituba moved the wheels of fate toward the ensuing witch trials. However, there were also many other subtle reasons which initiated the overwhelming fear and suspicion that ultimately culminated with the death of many.

POLITICAL PROBLEMS

Massachusetts was in a turbulent state not only religiously but also politically at the time of the Salem Witch Trials. Since the granting of its royal charter in 1629, the colony had had many periods of political unrest. However, the years immediately preceding the trials were the most traumatic.

On March 19, 1628, King Charles I granted a charter to John Endicott and six other individuals. Finally on March 4, 1629, a final charter was prepared which received the royal signature; thus, the settlement at Salem was officially recognized and was under the control of the Massachusetts Bay Company. After Endicott, John Winthrope was governor, and the most important political event under his administration was the removal of the government from mother country to New England. The legislature became colonial, and a corporation developed into a commonwealth.[34] The years between this period and 1684 were replete with political intrigue and skirmishes between Old and New England. Finally for a variety of reasons, the charter was annulled in October of 1684; she was no longer a chartered colony and had none of her former rights.[35] Sir Edmund Andros became governor in December 1686. However, after a rebellion he was deposed in 1689, and for the next two years Massachusetts was governed by a provisional government. In 1688, Increase Mather was sent to London as an agent for the colony and desired to have a restoration of the 1629 charter. Finally in 1691 after much debate, the King of England granted a new charter to Massachusetts and appointed William Phips as governor.[36]

The new charter had several restrictions. The people could not appoint the governor, but rather he was appointed by the crown. All laws passed by the legislature were to be sent to England for approval. In reality, the governor did not represent the people of Massachusetts but the King of England.[37] The new charter of 1691 changed the elective rights which Massachusetts citizens had experienced for fifty years. It allowed the governor greater power than he had ever experienced and created much dissension.[38]

Increase Mather, of course, was perhaps the most prominent religious figure in the Massachusetts Bay area. However, when he returned there was much opposition to him; this factious spirit mirrored the political chaos prevalent at this particular period. Increase Mather was opposed by two divergent groups. The conservatives were against him since they felt he was responsible for altering the terms of the franchise

THE CAUSES FOR THE BELIEF

from church membership to property qualifications. The liberals represented by William Brattle and John Leverett felt Mather was an unenlightened individual who stood in the way of progress.[39] There was a strong sense of social upheaval caused by the change in the charter. Lamprey writes:

> The Salem panic of 1692-1693, instead of being a popular outbreak of superstition and cruelty as generally supposed, occurred in an interval when the colony had lost its charter and Increase Mather and others in England were trying to get a new one.[40]

The period was very turbulent politically and there seemingly was a general feeling of hopelessness. Erikson writes:

> In many important respects, 1692 marked the end of the Puritan experiment in Massachusetts, not only because the original charter had been revoked ... or even because the old political order had collapsed in a tired heap. The Puritan experiment ended in 1692, rather because the sense of mission which had sustained it from the beginning no longer existed... and thus the people of the bay were left with a few stable points of reference to help them remember who they were.[41]

FEAR OF INDIANS

The Puritans believed that while God had led them to Massachusetts, it was a formidable land and one had to be on constant surveillance for the evil which lurked nearby. Cotton Mather wrote that the New Englanders were a people of God, settled in the devil's territories and that Satan was disturbed since there were many people who were believers in the gospel of Jesus Christ.[42] The atmosphere was set; they reasoned Satan and his forces were planning to subvert the Puritan empire, and his efforts had to be thwarted.

Massachusetts at this period primarily consisted of deep, dank forests which incited an atmosphere of dread and awe. Cultivation had only begun to make inroads; the vast majority of the land was shrouded in obscurity and believed to be unconquerable.[43] This was the habitat of the Indian. The Puritans did not understand him, and many believed the Indian was the cohort of Satan. The painted faces and pow-wows confirmed in the minds of the Puritans that they were in league with the forces of the netherworld. In the late 1680s, there was a great emphasis upon the person of Satan and his supposed messengers.[44] It was believed that Satan actually indwelt the Indian.

> The Puritans believed the Indians, like all unregenerate men, were in the clutches of Satan. Furthermore, there was a consensus among New Englanders that the natives actually sought comradeship with the devil and worshiped him.... The frequency of war scares in New England colonies convinced the Puritans that the Indians were in league with Satan.[45]

One of the tenets of witchcraft was that there would be a contract made with Satan himself.[46] With the prevalence of Indians and the belief that they were Satan's emissaries, it is apparent why the belief in witches was so prevalent.

THE CAUSES FOR THE BELIEF

In 1689 two people were killed by Indians in Salem, and in 1691 the county of Essex had twenty-four guards stationed to warn against an Indian raid. The inhabitants of Salem Village lived in constant fear for their safety.

> To them, he (the Indian) had become a frightful reality, a treacherous and unpitying foe, whose painted face and appalling whoop struck terror to the strongest heart....None knew when the fierce savage with horrid face ... might rush the man driving the plow in the field or fall upon the helpless wife and children at home.[47]

SOCIAL PROBLEMS

It has been seen that there were great social and psychological forces covertly and overtly occurring which had a profound effect upon the people of Salem. However, there were other problems concerning the people of Salem themselves. They were known for their contentiousness and inability to live in harmony with one another, especially their immediate neighbors. They gossiped constantly and quarrels would last for long periods of time.[48] Therefore, there was not only a suspicion and fear of witches and evil, but there was also great internal hostility, envy, and strife among the residents of Salem. As events progressed, the hostility toward one another and the great fear of the unknown merged until it was almost impossible to distinguish between the two. Actually, there were so many events occurring that it is difficult for one to see order in the kaleidoscope of events. Thwaites writes:

> There was general despondency in Massachusetts in 1692, the result of four small-pox epidemics which had quickly followed each other, the loss of the old charter, a temporary increase in crime, financial depression and general dread of another Indian outbreak. The time was ripe for an epidemic of superstitious fear.[49]

One reason for the great fear was seemingly a misunderstanding of one another. There were also many personal conflicts which contributed to a sense of mistrust for one another. Holliday cogently writes:

> There were also many personal grievances, petty jealousy...and neighborhood quarrels entered into the conflict; but the results were out of proportion to such causes, and remain today among the blackest and most sorrowful records on the pages of American history.[50]

Paul Boyer and Stephen Nissenbaum in their book, *Salem Possessed*, believe that the major factor for the accusations of various individuals was the result of a power struggle between the two most prominent families in Salem, the Porters and the Putnams. This seems, though, a simplification of the varied and complex sources for the actual trials; as previously displayed, there were a myriad of causes. The authors, though, have a sound understanding of the intense internal conflict occurring in Salem.

And of course, the witchcraft trials themselves offer the most per-

THE CAUSES FOR THE BELIEF

suasive evidence of the passionate emotions which underlay those longstanding divisions. To understand this intensity, we must recognize the fact ... that what was going on was not simply a personal quarrel, but a moral struggle involving the very nature of the community itself.[51]

There was, then, a struggle among the inhabitants themselves of Salem. The court records verify this as the courts were full of land disputes, personal feuds, and suits.[52]

Another problem concerned itself with a lack of constructive outlets for the children of Salem. The Puritans frowned upon frivolity, but the practicing of magic was something that was especially taboo since it represented the exact antithesis of what their culture was based upon. Perhaps one reason the séances in Reverend Parris' home had such a peculiar hold over the children was because it took them away from the routine of life offered by their culture. These clandestine meetings possibly were an expression of rebellion, consciously or unconsciously, against various characteristics of their culture. Fleming states concerning the plight of the children:

> Children suffered cruelly from the fear of sin's consequences. Sometimes their distress continued over a long period, during which they could get no peace. Apparently they were not helped by their elders, the latter being able only to counsel submission.[53]

It is apparent why the séances and the resulting accusations of various adults occurred; the children were given authority and status in the village. Those who claimed they had been afflicted by witchcraft were regarded as privileged individuals in Salem since it was believed that they had been chosen to have special knowledge of the supernatural. Physically sick people whom doctors could not help were brought to the children for consultation; there was status in their position.[54] It actually became in vogue to claim to have been bewitched or afflicted and then to accuse a certain individual of practicing witchcraft. There seemingly was a domino effect; one girl after another claimed to have been afflicted in some manner by an individual, and these accusations led to the trials themselves.

Chapter II

A BACKGROUND OF THE ACCUSERS AND THE ACCUSED

THE ACCUSERS

The primary witnesses were the young girls of the colony, and in particular those who had been associated with Tituba, the slave. Those who claimed to have been assaulted by witchcraft informed Samuel Parris who solicited the help of other ministers. Cotton Mather himself wrote how one knows Satan can molest innocent people. He gave six reasons. Three of these were Scripture, experience, and the testimony of learned men.[1] Betty Parris and Abigale Williams continued to experience their hysterical fits, and shortly thereafter their friends began to experience the same malady. Samuel Parris after much pressure decided to bring the matter to civil authorities. "On February 29, 1692, warrants went out for the arrest of three Village women whom the girls, under the pressure of intense adult questioning, had finally named as their tormentors: Sarah Good, Sarah Osburne, and Tituba herself."[2]

The Cry at Salem: America's Witchcraft Trials

There were many who witnessed that they had been bewitched or afflicted by various individuals. The leading accuser was Elizabeth Parris, daughter of Reverend Samuel Parris. She was active in the initial stages of the accusations, but when the trials began her father sent her away. Abigale Williams, Samuel Parris's eleven-year-old niece, was one of the primary witnesses since she was active throughout the trials. The major witness was Ann Putnam, age twelve, daughter of Thomas Putnam, and belonging to one of Salem's most prominent families. She was a very precocious child with a vivid imagination, and her accusations captivated the crowds during the many court sessions. Mary Walcot and Mercy Lewis, both seventeen, were major witnesses; the latter, however, was more active. Elizabeth Hubbard, seventeen, and Elizabeth Booth and Susannah Sheldon, both eighteen, took an active role. There were other "afflicted" who also took a role in accusing various individuals or who claimed that they themselves were tormented; however, their names were not listed in court records. There were also three married women who joined the children and presented their own accusations. These were Mrs. Ann Putnam, Mrs. Pope, and a woman named Goodell.[3] Tituba also accused various individuals of witchcraft, and her accusations seemingly made a marked impression upon the court. The so-called "tall man of Boston" also confirmed their fears that outside forces were closing in on their kingdom. Even though Tituba herself was accused of witchcraft, she charged others of the same crime.

The questioning of Tituba by John Hathorne was extensive and the questions pointed.

> The examination of Titibe [*sic*].
> (H) Titibe what evil spirit have you familiarity with.

A Background of the Accusers and the Accused

(T) none.

(H) why do you hurt these children.

(T) I do not hurt them.

(H) who is it then.

(T) the devil for ought I know.

(H) Did you ever see the devil.

(T) The devil came to me and bid me serve him.

(H) Who have you seen.

(T) Four women who sometimes hurt the children.

(H) Who were they.

(T) Goode Osburn and Sarah Good and I do not know who the other were. Sarah Good and Osburne would have me hurt the children but I would not she further saith there was a tall man of Boston that she did not see....[4]

Ann Putnam's testimonial against Sarah Good went as follows:

The Deposition of Ann Putnam Jur who testifieth and saith, that on the 25th of February 1691/92 I saw the Apperishtion of Sarah Good which did tortor me most greviously, but I did not know her name tell the 27th of February and then she told me hir name was Sarah Good and then she did prick me and pinch me most greviously, and also sence ... the first day of March ... did mot greviosly tortor me....I saw the Apperishtion of Sarah Good goe and afflect and tortor the bodys of Elizabeth Parish and Abigail Williams and Elizabeth Hubbard.[5]

Elizabeth Hubbard brought these words against Sarah Osburne:

I saw the Apperishtion of Sarah Osborn the wife of Alexander
Osborn who did most greviously tortor me by pricking and pinching me most dreadfully and so she continued hurting me most greviously tell the first of March 1691/92 being the day of hir
Examination and then also Sarah Osborn did tortor me most greviously by pinching and pricking me most dreadfully and also severall times since Sarah Osborn has afflected me and urged me to
write in hir book.[6]

Abigale Williams also brought charges against three individuals.

The testimony of Abigail Williams testifyeth and saith that severall
times last February she hath been much afflicted with pains in her
head and other parts and often pinched by the apparition of Sarah
Good, Sarah Osburne, an Tituba Indian all of Salem Village, and also
excessively afflicted by the said apparition of said Good Osburne
and Tituba at their examination before authority the 1st of March
last part 169 1/2.[7]

Mary Walcot's testimony is as follows:

I saw the Apperishtion of Dorothy Good. Sarah Goods daughter
com to me and bit me, and pinch me and so she continued afflect-
ing me by times tell the 24 March being the day of hir examination
and then she did torment and afflect me most greviously during
the time to the examination and also severall times sence the
Apperishtion of Dorothy Good has afflected me by biting pinching
and almost choaking me, urging me to writ in hir book.[8]

A BACKGROUND OF THE ACCUSERS AND THE ACCUSED

Abigale Williams testified against Rebecca Nurse:

> The testimony of Abigale Williams witnesseth and saith that divers times in the month of March last past particularly on the 15. 16. 19. 20. 21. 23. 31 days of that month and in the month of April following at severall times, particularly on the 13. & 1* of that month, and also in the present month of May, the 4th and 29 days she the said Abigale has been exceedingly perplexed with the apparition of Rebeka Nurse of Salem Village, by which apparition she hath been pulled violently and often pinched and almost choked and tempted sometimes to leap onto the fire and sometimes to subscribe to a book the said apparition brought... and further saith that said apparition hath sometimes confessed to her the said Abigale its guilt in committing several murders together with her sister Cloyse.... Abigale Williams did owne this har testimony on the oath which she hath taken, to be the truth before us the Juriars of Inquest the 3. day of June:92.[9]

One begins to notice a pattern in all the accusations; many of the witnesses described their afflictions in similar terms. Booth believes many accused others as witches in order that they themselves would not be accused.[10] The Puritans, of course, were aware of the need for educating their children, and this they did thoroughly. Of the eight major witnesses, though, only two could write their names.[11] While this does not necessarily reflect their native intelligence, it seems odd that in such a well-educated society some of the poorest educated had great prestige.

THE ACCUSED

Between May and September 1692, hundreds were arrested on charges of witchcraft.[12] A much smaller number met their deaths: nineteen were hanged, one was pressed to death, and two died in jail. Some of the accused people began to believe that they themselves actually were witches. They were vehemently accused and without any real chance to testify for themselves; therefore, some accepted the testimonies of others against them as valid. If one confessed he or she could escape execution and actually earn the respect of the judges since it was assumed that the accused could point out the others who supposedly helped them.[13] A woman named Deliverance Hobbs was examined by Judge Hathorne and admitted she was a witch who delighted in hurting the children. Rebecca Nurse did not give a strong account of herself at her questioning, and she was one of the unfortunate to be hanged. A woman named Martha Corey also condemned herself. She was highly skeptical toward the idea that there were witches. This was considered blasphemous because it was contrary to what Puritan doctrine stated. A warrant was later issued against her. The entire basis, then, for accusing people was totally unjustified. The people began looking for evidences of guilt and not innocence; they could no longer perceive good in anyone.[14]

It is beyond the scope of this book to investigate the trial proceedings of all who were accused of witchcraft; thus, the viewing of the cases will have to be limited. The first two to be examined in this book are Sarah Good and Sarah Osburne. They were sent to Boston and impris-

A Background of the Accusers and the Accused

oned. Two months later Sarah Osburne died there in prison while a baby born to Sarah Good met the same fate.[15]

Sarah Good was somewhat of a peculiar person; she was disliked by most people in the community.[16] Upham states:

> There was a general readiness to receive the charge against her, as she was evidently the object of much prejudice in the neighborhood. Her husband, who was a weak, ignorant and dependent person, had become alienated from her. The family were very poor, and she and her children had sometimes been without a house to shelter them, and left to wander from door to door for relief. Whether justly or not, she appears to have been subject to general obloquy. Probably there was no one in the country around, against whom popular suspicion could have been more readily directed, or in whose favor and defense less interest could be awakened.[17]

Sarah Good's examination is as follows:

> The examination of Sarah Good before the worshipfull Assts. John Hathorn Jonathan Curran
>
> > (H) Sarah Good what evil Spirit have you familiarity with
> >
> > (SG) None
> >
> > (H) Have you made no contracte with the devil
> >
> > Good answered no.
> >
> > (H) Why doe you hurt these children
> >
> > (O) I doe not hurt them. I scorn it.
> >
> > (H) Who doe you imploy then to doe it.

(g) I imploy no body

(H) What creature do you imploy then.

(g) no creature but I am falsely accused.

(H) Why did you go away muttering from Mr. Parris his house.

(g) I did not mutter but I thanked him for what he gave my child.

(H) have you made no contract with the devil.

(g) no...

(H) Sarah Good do you not see now what you have done, why doe you not tell us the truth, why doe you thus torment these poor children

(g) I doe not torment them.

(H) who do you imploy then.

(g) I imploy nobody I scorn it ...

(H) who doe you serve

(g) I serve God

(H) what God doe you serve.

(g) the God that made heaven and earth....

Salem Village March the 1st 169 1/2.[18]

Sarah Good was sent to the gallows on July 10; however, not without having the last word.

> At Execution, Mr. Noyes urged Sarah Good to Confess, and told her she was a Witch, and she knew she was a Witch, to which she replied, you are a lyar, I am no more a Witch than you are a Wizard, and if you take away my Life, God will give you Blood to drink.[19]

A Background of the Accusers and the Accused

Sarah Osborne was accused of witchcraft by several individuals. She had already been involved in somewhat of a scandal as she had lived with her husband before marriage.[20] Sarah Osburne was about sixty years old at the time of the trials. She came from Ireland a few years before the trials; however, she was sickly and spent much of her time confined in bed.[21] After Sarah Good was examined, the magistrate informed Sarah Osburne that Good had confessed and accused her of witchcraft. This was a lie, but it displays the devious tactics of the magistrates at the trials. Sarah Osburne, though, maintained her innocence throughout her questioning and subsequent imprisonment.

Her examination is as follows:

(H) what evil spirit have you familiarity with

(O) none.

(H) have you made no contract with the devill.

(O) no I never saw the devill in my life.

(H) why doe you hurt these children.

(O) I doe not hurt them.....

(H) Sarah Good saith that it was you that hurt the children.

(O) I doe not know that the devil goes about in my likeness to doe any hurt....

(H) what lying spirit is this, hath the devil ever deceived you nd been false to you.

(O) I doe not know the devil I never did see him.

(H) what lying spirit was it then.

(O) it was a voice I thought I heard.

(H) what did it propound to you.

(O) that I should goe no more to meeting, but I said I would and did goe the next Sabbath day.
(H) were you never tempted further.
(O) no.[22]

An interesting accusation was that of Rebecca Nurse. Ann Putnam claimed that she was bitten by her. After Nurse had been placed in jail several miles away from Ann Putnam, the latter claimed Nurse struck her several times with a chain.[23] Rebecca Nurse was seventy-one years of age at the witchcraft trials. She and her husband became involved in a land dispute with Nathaniel Putnam, and the affair developed into a lawsuit. It was the same Putnam family that accused her of witchcraft and brought about her examination on March 24.[24] The magistrates were deeply confused concerning the accusation of Rebecca Nurse for witchcraft. She was considered to be a godly individual, and they viewed her as an unlikely candidate for witchcraft.[25]

The summons against Rebecca Nurse is as follows:

> William and Mary by ye Grace of God of England &c.
> To Abigail Williams Ann Putnam Mercy Lewis, Elizabeth Hubbard, Mary Walcott, Ann Putnam senr. Susanna Sheldon, will command that they and every of them all excuses set aside appear before theire Maj'ties Justices of Court of Oyer and Terminer Holden this present Thursday being 2d of June. at eight of ye clock in ye morning to Testifie ye truth of what they know, upon certain Endictments Exhibited at our sd Court on behalfe of our Sovereigne agt. Rebecka Nurse here of fail not at your perill, and make return.

A BACKGROUND OF THE ACCUSERS AND THE ACCUSED

Stephen Sewall, cler

To ye Constable of Salem.[26]

The examination of Rebecca Nurse is interesting and is as follows:

The examination of Rebecka Nurse at Salem Village 24. Mar. 1692,

Mr. Harthorn. What do you say (speaking to one afflicted) have you seen this woman hurt you,

yes, she beat me this morning

Abigail. have you ben hurt by this woman?

Yes.

Ann Putnam in a grevous fit cryed out that she hurt her.

Goody Nurse: here are two: Ann Putnam the child and Abigail Williams, complains of your hurting them. What do you say to it?

N. I can say before my Eternal Father I am innocent and God will clear my innocency.

Here is never a one in the Assembly but desires it. but if you be Guilty Pray God discover you....

N. I am innocent and clear, and have not been able to get out of doors these 8. or 9. dayes....

You do Know whether you are Guilty and have familiarity with the devil, and now when you are here present, to see such a thing as these testify a black man whispering in your ear and birds about you, what do you say to it.

It is all false. I am clear.[27]

The jury returned a verdict of not guilty on June 28, but as soon as they did the accusers began rolling on the floor and crying out their disapproval of the verdict. The jury decided to meet again, and when they returned they still could not come to a conclusion. They then asked her about a remark made by a confessing witch, Abigale Hobbs, who stated that Rebecca Nurse was "one of us." Actually, Hobbs meant she was one of the accused and not specifically a witch; the jury though understood it as an accusation of witchcraft. The jury asked Rebecca Nurse concerning this remark, but she did not answer. A verdict of guilty was returned, however, when told that her silence was what condemned her, she explained in amazement that she did not hear the question since she was somewhat deaf and that was the reason she did not answer.[28] Her explanation was to no avail, and she was sent to the gallows and hanged on July 19.

Susannah Martin was a widow and was accused of witchcraft as early as 1669 but had managed to escape conviction. Later a neighbor claimed Susannah Martin was a witch because she had seen the latter walk through a storm without getting wet.[29] A John Atkinson testified that

> He exchanged a cow with a Son of Susanna Martin's whereat she muttered, and was unwilling he should have it. Going to receive this cow, tho' he Hamstringe' her, and Halter'd her, she, of a Tame Creature, grew so mad, that they could scarce get her along. She broke all the Ropes that were fastned unto her, and though she were ty'd fast unto a Tree, yet she made her escape, and gave them such further trouble, as they could ascribe to no cause but Witchcraft.[30]

A Background of the Accusers and the Accused

Her examination is as follows:

> The examination of Susannah Martin 2. May 1692.
>
> As soon as she came into the meeting house many fell into fits.
>
> Hath this woman hurt you?
>
> Abig: Williams saith it is Goody Martin she hath hurt me often. Others by fits were hindred from speaking.
>
> Eliz: Hubbard said she had not hurt her. John Indian said he never saw her
>
> Mercy Lewis pointed at her and fell into a fit. Ann Putnam threw her glove in a fit at her.
>
> Why do you laugh at it?
>
> Will I may at such folly.
>
> Is this folly to see these so hurt?
>
> I never hurt man woman or child.... I have no hand in witchcraft.
>
> What did you do? Did you consent these should be hurt?
>
> No never in my life.
>
> What ails these people?
>
> I do not know.
>
> But what do you think ails them?
>
> I do not desire to spend my judgment upon it.
>
> Do you think they are bewitcht?
>
> No I do not think they are....
>
> What have you done towards the hurt of these?
>
> I have done nothing....
>
> I desire to lead my life according to the word of God....

The Cry at Salem: America's Witchcraft Trials

Do you not see God evidently discovering you?

No, not a bit for that.

All the congregation besides think so.

Let them think what they will.

What is the reason these cannot come to You?

I do not know but they can if they will or else if you please I will come to them.

What was that the black man whispered to you?

There was none whispered to me.[31]

Susannah Martin was found guilty of witchcraft and was hanged on July 19.

One of the last individuals to be tried and hanged was Mary Easty. She was the sister of Rebecca Nurse, and at her first examination on April 22, she had so impressed the judge as innocent that he doubted the girls' accusations. She was released on May 18, but immediately she was accused by Mercy Lewis of choking.[32] There were many complaints against Mary Easty. One of the more interesting is as follows:

> The deposition of Jonathan Putnam, James Darling, Benja Hutchinson & Sam: Baybrook to testify and say that we together with divers others the 20: May, 1692. between eight and eleven oclock at night being with Mercy Lewes whom we found as if death would have quickly followed, and to whom Eliz: Hubbard was brought (said Mercy being unable to speak most of the day) to discover what she could see did afflict said Mercy, heard and observed that these two fell into fits by turns. The one being well whilst the other was ill, and that each of them complained much of Mary Eastie, who brought the book to said Mercy severall times

A Background of the Accusers and the Accused

as we heard her say in her trances, and vexed and tortured them both.[33]

She was examined on April 22.

The Examination of Mary Eastie.
At a court held at Salem village 22:Apr. 1692.
By the Wop. John Hathorne & Jonathan Corwin.
At the bringing in of the accused severall fell into fits.
Doth this woman hurt you.
Many mouths were stopt, and several other fits seized them.
Abig: Williams said it was Goody Eastie, and she had hurt her, the like said Mary Walcot & Ann Putnam, John Jackson said he saw her with Goody Hobbs.
What do you say, are you guilty?
I can say before Christ Jesus, I am free....
What have you done to these children?
I know nothing.
How can you say you know nothing, when you see these tormented, and accuse you that you know nothing?
Would you have me accuse myself?
Yes if you be guilty....
How far have you complyed with Satan whereby he takes this advantage at you?
Sir, I never complyed but prayed against him all my dayes. I have no compliance with Satan, in this. What would you have me to do?
Confess if you be guilty.
I will say it, if it was my last time, I am clear of this sin.

THE CRY AT SALEM: AMERICA'S WITCHCRAFT TRIALS

Of what sin?

Of witchcraft.[34]

Before Mary Easty's death she posted the following petition:

> To the Honorable Judge and Bench now sitting in judicature in Salem and the Reverend Ministers, humbly sheweth, that whereas your humble poor Petitioner being condemned to die, doth humbly beg of you, to take it into your Judicious and Pious consideration that your poor and humble Petitioner knowing my own Innocency (Blessed by the Lord for it) and seeing plainly the Wiles and Subtilty of my Accusers.... I Petition to your Honours not for my own life, for know I must die, and my appointed time is set; but the Lord he knows it is, if it be possible, that no more innocent blood be shed....They say, my self and others have made a league with the Devil, we cannot confess I know and the Lord he knows (as will shortly appear).... I beg your Honours not to deny this my humble Petition, from a poor dying Innocent person, and I question not but the Lord will give a blessing to your Endeavors.[35]

The last individual to be a victim of the Salem witch trials was Giles Corey. The method putting him to death was vastly different that the other nineteen who were hanged. After being accused by several individuals, he was brought to court on September 17. However, when questioned what was his plea, he did not reply. According to colonial law an individual who stood mute could not be tried but could be tortured. He was taken to a gathering place and laid on the ground and large stones were placed on his chest. With each additional stone many begged him to talk, but he refused; he died after two days of such treatment.[36]

A BACKGROUND OF THE ACCUSERS AND THE ACCUSED

The following account of Giles Corey is contained in Samuel Sewell's personal diary:

> Monday, Sept. 19, 1692. About noon, at Salem, Giles Corey was pressed to death for standing Mute; much pains was used with him two days, one after another, by the Court and Capt. Gardner of Nantucket who had been of his acquaintance: but all in vain.[37]

In summary, there was a total of twenty-two who met their deaths; nineteen were hanged, one was pressed to death, and two died in prison. The life of Bridget Bishop was taken on June 10. On July 19, 1692 five were hanged: Sarah Good, Rebecca Nurse, Susannah Martin, Elizabeth Howe, and Sarah Wildes. A month later on August 19, five more were sent to the gallows: John Proctor (his wife, Elizabeth Proctor, was also condemned but given a stay of execution until after her baby's birth), John Willard, George Jacobs, Martha Carrier, and George Burroughs. Eight met their deaths on September 22 including Martha Corey, Mary Easty, Alice Parker, Ann Pudeator, Margaret Scott, Wilmot Read, Samuel Wardwell, and Mary Parker. Giles Corey died September 19, and Sarah Osburne and a small baby died in jail at Boston.

ACCUSATIONS: JUSTIFIED OR BIASED

One must realize that the people involved with the Salem witch trials were individuals influenced by the thinking and historical currents of their own period. Therefore, in a sense it is impossible for anyone to condemn them. However toward the end of the trials and immediately following them, many influential people expressed remorse for accusing various individuals and participating actively in the trials. Judge Samuel Sewall, a prominent judge in the trials, publicly asked for forgiveness. One can come to the conclusion then, that even though they were persons of their times, the inhabitants of Salem were enlightened enough to see that there was something grossly wrong with the method used of accusing various individuals as witches.

The vast majority of the accusations could not be justified. Some stemmed from the fact that the younger girls had a natural aversion toward the older, unkempt country women. These women were known to slaughter pigs, work in mud and speak roughly and harshly to the young mischievous girls of the community.[38] In order to be objective, one cannot rule out entirely the supernatural. There was indeed some clear and valid evidence of witchcraft in Salem. A woman named Candy from Barbados admitted she had been practicing voodoo, and an individual named Mammy Reed also admitted her use of black magic.[39] The premise that the accused were demons or were possessed by demons is greatly diminished when one studies the manner in which the accusations were performed and comes to understand the social and psychological forces which resulted into the trials conducted in Salem.

Many accused various individuals as witches primarily so that they themselves would not be charged.[40] If one admitted to witchcraft, all charges would be dropped. Clark cogently writes, "Tragically all of those who were executed were honest people who simply refused to survive by lying, by falsely confessing to the charges of witchcraft."[41]

A Background of the Accusers and the Accused

It is difficult not to be skeptical when one views the manner in which the accusations were effected. When one objectively views the data, he or she will come to the conclusion that the accusations were biased and many totally unjustified. The girls seemingly would attempt to outdo the other in the method of charging various people. Some of the girls would gnash their teeth and roll on the floor before the accused; they would claim the latter were afflicting them and causing their fits. Oberholzer claims the girls learned the method of simulating fits from Tituba.[42] As soon as the defendant was brought in the courtroom the girls claimed they were being afflicted. They would begin their antics, and to the horror of the crowded courtroom they would point fingers at various individuals. Upham sums up well the accusers:

> Whatever opinion may be formed of the moral or mental condition of the afflicted children, as to the sanity or responsibility, there can be no doubt that they were great actors. In mere jugglery and sleight of hand, they bear no mean comparison with the workers of wonders, in that line, of our own day. Long practice had given them complete control over their countenances, intonation of voice, and the entire muscular and nervous organization of their bodies; so that they could at will, and on the instant go into fits and convulsions, swoon and fall to the floor.[43]

The Cry at Salem: America's Witchcraft Trials

Chapter III

STATISTICS AND TRAITS OF INDIVIDUALS INVOLVED WITH THE SALEM WITCH TRIALS

The vast majority of those accused were innocent of such charges. Many of the accusations grew out of the great fear and tension prevalent in Salem. Others were charged either because they acted in a peculiar manner or had a neighbor who desired to "get even" with them. Most of the accused came from the lower class; however, the really common factor was that they were considered eccentric or deviant in some manner. Some were known as fortune tellers while others exhibited criminal behavior such as robbery and battery. Most were considered contentious and quarrelsome.[1]

STATISTICS

The following are statistics of people accused of witchcraft in Salem. The records from which these statistics are taken contain discrepancies, and no reason is given for these variations.

TABLE 1
MARITAL STATUS OF THE ACCUSED

SEX	TOTAL	MARITAL STATUS	MALE	FEMALE	TOTAL
Male	42	Single	8	29	37
Female	120	Married	15	61	76
		Widowed	1	20	21
Total	162	Total	24	110	134

Source: John Demos, "Underlying Themes in the Witchcraft of Seventeenth Century New England," *American Historical Review* 75 (June 1970):1315.

TABLE 2
AGE OF THE ACCUSED

AGE	MALE	FEMALE	TOTAL
Under 20	3	7	10
21-30	6	18	24
31-40	3	8	11
41-50	6	18	24
51-60	5	23	28
61-70	4	8	12
Over 70	3	6	9
Total	30	88	118

Source: Demos, "Underlying Themes in the Witchcraft of Seventeenth Century New England," p. 1315.

Most of the accused witches were married or widowed and were between the ages of forty-one and sixty. An official statement concerning whether a person was a witch or not read:

STATISTICS AND TRAITS OF INDIVIDUALS

If ye party suspect be ye son or daughter... or familiar friend; neer neighbor or old companion of a knowne or convicted witch this also a presumption for witchcraft... oft it falleth out yet a witch dying leaveth some of ye aforesd heirs of her witchcraft.[2]

Almost one hundred percent of the young men who were executed were accused were charged because of their convicted mothers or wives since it was believed witchcraft was communicable.[3]

The primary witnesses exhibited strange behavior which included shaking and in more extreme cases rolling on the floor and convulsions. The majority of the witnesses who exhibited deviant behavior were young women between the ages of eleven and twenty. In all, there were eighty-four witnesses.

TABLE 3
THE MARITAL STATUS OF THE WITNESSES WHO EXHIBITED DEVIANT BEHAVIOR

Sex	Total	Marital Status	Male	Female	Total
Male	5	Single	5	23	28
Female	29	Married	0	6	6
		Widowed	0	0	0
Total	34	Total	5	29	34

Source: Demos, "Underlying Themes in the Witchcraft of Seventeenth Century New England," p. 1315.

TABLE 4
MARITAL STATUS OF THE WITNESSES

Sex	Total	Marital Status	Male	Female	Total
Male	63	Single	11	3	14
Female	21	Married	39	16	55
		Widowed	3	1	4
Total	84	Total	53	20	73

Source: Demos, "Underlying themes in the Witchcraft of Seventeenth Century New England," p. 1316.

In the following table, notice the broad distribution in ages of the witnesses. This proves that all, not just a certain group, believed in witchcraft in Salem.

TABLE 5
THE AGE OF THE WITNESSES

Age	Male	Female	Total
Under 20	3	2	5
21-30	13	4	17
31-40	14	6	20
41-50	18	7	25
51-60	11	1	12
61-70	2	1	3
Over 70	2	0	2
Total	63	21	84

Source: Demos, "Underlying Themes in the Witchcraft of Seventeenth Century New England," p. 1316.

STATISTICS AND TRAITS OF INDIVIDUALS

TRAITS

APPEARANCE AND PERSONALITY

As previously stated, many of those charged with witchcraft were considered peculiar or strange in some manner. For example, Sarah Good was idle and unkempt. She begged for food, smoked a pipe, and was very "haggy" looking.[4] Wright cogently states concerning the ensuing witchcraft trials: "By this time the whole community was aflamed with talk about witches and no eccentric old woman or man was safe from suspicion."[5]

Bridget Bishop seemingly was charged with witchcraft primarily because of her seductive-like tendencies. She was a flashy dresser and especially delighted in wearing elaborate laces. As a tavern keeper, she would allow young men to loiter until late hours, and at times such an uproar would be made that the neighbors' sleep was disturbed.[6] Samuel Gray was one of the primary witnesses against Bridget Bishop, and on his death bed he recanted and claimed such accusations had no basis.

> Upon his death-bed he testified his sorrow and repentance for such Accusations, as being wholly groundless; yet the report taken up by his means continued, and she being accused by the afflicted.... She was brought in guilty by the jury; she received her Sentence of Death, and was executed, June 10, but made not the

least confession of anything relating to witchcraft.[7]

Susannah Martin had for a long period been charged with witchcraft. Rather than being strange or different, she seemingly invoked the hostility of her neighbors by her domineering personality. Speaking of Susannah Martin, Drake states:

> She belonged to Amesbury and appears to have been a woman of great spirit and business Capacity, and perhaps somewhat prone to wordy Contests, by which she had excited the Jealousy of envious Neighbors. Her trial took place on the 29th of June, in which she was found guilty, and was hanged on the 19th of July following. At her examination her replies to the Judge's Questions show a mind far superior to that of the court; and for Directness, Conciseness, and common Sense, had commended itself to all Readers from that Day to this.[8]

George Burroughs, a former minister of Salem from 1680-1682, was summoned to court and hanged on August 19. He seemingly was an extremely strong man even though not especially well-built. It was known that he could lift a heavy gun simply by placing his finger in the muzzle.[9] This was considered incredible since the gun was very heavy; thus, he was suspected of being in league with witchcraft. It was considered impossible for an individual connected with witchcraft to repeat the Lord's Prayer. George Burroughs, however, achieved this at his execution, but his life still was not spared. Upham writes concerning this event:

> Mr. Burroughs was carried in a cart with the others, through the

streets of Salem to execution. When he was upon the ladder, he made a speech for the clearing of his innocency, with such solemn and serious expressions as were to the admiration of all present. His prayer (which he concluded by repeating the Lord's Prayer) was so well worded .... that it seemed to some that the spectators would hinder the execution. The accusers said the black man stood and dictated to him. As soon as he was turned off Mr. Cotton Mather ... addressed himself to the people saying the Devil often had been transformed into an angel of light ... and the execution went on.[10]

Not all who were charged with witchcraft were considered eccentric or strange. Martha Corey was a woman greatly respected among the older people of the village. However, she incurred the disfavor of the children by possessing a somewhat condescending attitude toward them. Boyer claims that one reason she was charged with witchcraft was because of a mistake she had made many years before: she gave birth to an illegitimate mulatto son.[11] Mrs. Corey's husband also testified against her by stating she had been acting in a peculiar manner and had been reading strange books.[12] However, even though she was accused by her own husband and had an illegitimate son, Martha Corey remained a respected person among the older citizens of Salem. Her mistake was that she stirred up the children's wrath by a displeasing attitude toward them; thus, she was shortly charged with witchcraft.

Wilmot Reed had long been considered a witch, but her neighbors never thought of pressing charges against her. She apparently was considered somewhat strange but of no threat. Her problem began when she became involved in a quarrel with a Mrs. Simms, and the latter threatened to swear out a warrant against her. Wilmot Reed proceeded to pronounce a curse that Mrs. Simms "might never mingere (urinate) nor cacare (defecate)."[13] Two witnesses heard the words, and of course in their minds this confirmed she was a witch. She was hanged on September 22.

Social Class

There was a definite division of people into various classes in Salem, and there were many ways that class distinction was shown. The order on college lists, methods of seating in churches, and the titles ranging from "goodman" to "esquire" depicted the Puritan's method of elevating certain individuals. In 1651 Massachusetts passed a law stating the wearing of such finery as gold, silver, lace and silk must be limited to those whose estates were greater than two hundred pounds.[14] Jones states concerning the division: "New England social theory with its stratification of mankind into fixed classes, held that some were born aristocrats and rulers."[15] As previously stated, most of the accused came from the lower classes.

> It requires no Flexibility of Imagination to presume that many Families had been utterly ruined. The Imprisoned were generally persons of small Estates, and small as they were, Confiscation fell upon them. Besides that Besom of Destruction, Jailors Fees and Court Expenses were added to their Burthens.[16]

STATISTICS AND TRAITS OF INDIVIDUALS

As the witchcraft trials proceeded, the children began to charge some of the more respected and higher class citizens of the colony rather than the eccentric or "down and outers." One of the major reasons for the demise of the trials was because people began to question the validity of any of the accusations when many fine and respected individuals were placed under suspicion.

> At the end of this strenuous period of justice, the whole witch mania began to fade. For one thing the people of the Bay had been shocked into a mood of sober reflections by the deaths of so many persons. It was bad enough that they should accuse the likes of John Alden ... but when they brought up the name of Samuel Willard, who doubled as pastor of Boston's First Church and President of Harvard College, the magistrates told them they were mistaken.[17]

People became critical of the proceedings as many prominent individuals were charged. For example, one of the magistrates, Dudley Bradstreet, was accused and Mrs. Hale, pious wife of Reverend John Hale, was also charged. Perhaps the greatest mistake of the children was to charge Governor Phip's wife as a witch.[18]

The children seemingly became totally irrational in their accusations. Not content to charge individuals of lesser means, they incriminated people who were considered of excellent character. Demos believes the problem was primarily interpersonal rather than demonic.

> Most striking of all is the absence of allusions to sex; there is no nakedness, no promiscuity, no obscene contact with the Devil. This

seems to provide strong support for the general proposition that the psychological conflicts underlying the belief in witchcraft in early New England had much more to do with aggressive impulses rather than libidinal ones.[19]

Chapter IV

The Trial System of the Salem Witch Trials

The trial system cannot be considered valid by twenty-first century standards; however, to those in the seventeenth century it was fair. One must realize there is a steady progression of sophistication and knowledge in every field. The people in New England performed the best they could with their system, but it was definitely inferior. It was believed during this period that if one had pneumonia or a severe cold, one should drain the blood for a period of time. Their primitive medical methods somewhat correspond to their unsophisticated law system. They believed anyone who had allowed Satan to possess him or her in an extreme manner should be put to death.[1]

The Court of Oyer and Terminer

There were seven judges appointed to the court of Oyer and Terminer. These included Samuel Sewall, John Richards, William Sergeant,

THE CRY AT SALEM: AMERICA'S WITCHCRAFT TRIALS

Wait Winthrop, Nathaniel Saltonstall, Bartholomew Gedney, and the presiding justice, Deputy Governor Stoughton.[2] Of the presiding judges, two had been educated for the pulpit, two were physicians, one a merchant, and one a lawyer.[3] Men were appointed judges by their reputation and ability. William Stoughton led in the prosecution, and throughout the proceedings he never faltered from the conclusion that the charged were witches.[4] There was a jury, too, and their primary qualification was to be "good men."[5]

The court's rationale seemingly was that individuals of a tarnished reputation were surely guilty. Their guilt, then, was presupposed for they were constantly asked why they had hurt or afflicted various individuals.[6] The first session was held in Salem on Friday, June 2, 1692. The court met again on June 29 and continued through the fall of the same year. It might seem strange why there was no political intervention or advice in the Salem Witch Trials. The reason for this is that Governor Phips maintained a passive attitude. Nevins writes: "There is evidence that Gov. Phips was never in full sympathy with the mode of procedure in the witchcraft prosecutions. Being unlearned in law and theology, he seems to have followed the advice of the judges."[7]

Cotton Mather seemingly began to have doubts about the validity of witchcraft, and he agreed with Michael Wigglesworth that many innocent people had been put to death.[8]

The Trial System of the Salem Witch Trials

The Role of the Clergy and Judges

The clergy was considered the authority on witchcraft matters. Judge John Richards asked Cotton Mather to give some of his views. He claimed that devils afflicted men willfully.

> In all of witchcraft which now grievously vexes us, I know not whether anything be more unaccountable that the trick which the witches have, to render themselves and their tools invisible. Witchcraft seems to be the skill of applying the plastic spirit of the world unto some unlawful purposes, by a means of confederacy with evil spirits.[9]

After their first sentence, the court, though supported in their procedure by English precedents, showed a considerable interest in informing themselves as to the propriety of their course; therefore, they sought the advice of the clergy.[10]

The clergy looked for spiritual causes while the justices believed more tangible causes, specifically Spectral Evidence, were to be considered. The clergy seemed to never totally accept this type of evidence.

> There was a revulsion of the public mind against capital convictions for witchcraft. There was a growing feeling that "Spectral Evidence" was a delusion. The Ministers seeing that persons were condemned on such evidence, were more willing to have all judicial proceedings stayed.[11]

According to Samuel Mather, though, Cotton Mather respected the judges. "Nevertheless, on the other side, he saw in the most of the judges a charming instance of prudence and Patience; as he knew their exemplary piety, so he observed the agony of soul with which they sought the Direction of Heaven."[12]

The ministers in the eyes of many were not capable to judge since they had their own biases. Ziff writes:

> They were unable, however, to disengage themselves from the consequences of a stereotype they had promulgated, without denying its validity, and this they were emotionally uncapable of doing even when, occasionally, they were intellectually equipped to do it.[13]

However, many also believed ministers were superior. "Indeed as the law based itself on the Jewish Scriptures, Ministers, not Lawyers, were the best expounders of the same and the commonlaw of England was at a discount."[14]

The feud was not limited to just the clergy and the legal profession. Many doctors believed it was primarily a physical problem. Dr. John Cotta, a Northampton physician, claimed only those who had medical knowledge should judge the accused. He believed ministers alone could not adequately judge such a problem.[15] Cotton Mather, even though an astute clergyman, seemingly favored a combination of the spiritual, legal and physical. He believed "witchcraft was spiritual,, but the effects of it were dreadfully physical and punishable at law."[16] Perhaps the spiritual had priority over the legal; instead of being tried in a civil building, the trials were performed in a church.[17]

The Trial System of the Salem Witch Trials

The court cases were heard by assistant members of the general court of the colony. They did not have lawyers since it was believed all must submit to God. The English concept that one is not guilty until proven otherwise had no bearing. Most important, the judge was not bound by the decision of the jury.[18] In order to prepare themselves for the trials, the justices gathered books related to witchcraft and the supernatural. They also sent out a request to local ministers to explain their position on witchcraft and the procedure which should be taken in the actual trials.[19] Toward the end of the trials the judges had a change of heart. "A little later the judges who had been engaged in the trials began to make confession of their folly.... The jurors also began to regain their senses, and to confess that they were guilty of the blood of innocent neighbors."[20]

Confession

Confession was one of the primary methods for determining if one were guilty. Other methods included failure to recite the Lord's Prayer, testimony of the afflicted against the accused, physical imperfections through which the devil sucked blood, and spectral evidence.[21] Confession, however, was different from the other means of determining if one were a witch or not. If a person confessed, he or she would be free of the death penalty. There were many who "confessed" to witchcraft; those who did were received with sympathy and understanding.[22] Those who were charged with witchcraft found themselves in a dilemma.

An accused person was faced with the bitter choice of calling the accusation lies (which was just what a witch would do according to the judges) or of saving his own life by confessing his own guilt and nameing [*sic*] someone else as a fellow witch.[23]

Boyer and Nissenbaum believe the act of confession was a "ritual"of therapeutic value. They believe that there was such social turmoil between some of the Salem citizens that the onlookers themselves received great satisfaction when someone "confessed" to witchcraft. Many onlookers by projection were relieved of their own guilt caused by a general dislike of a certain neighbor or acquaintance. Thus, there was great social and psychological pressure placed upon those charged with witchcraft to make a statement of confession.[24]

Spectral Evidence

Spectral evidence was the most important evidence accepted by the judges as proof that one was a witch. The concept was that the devil would not assume the form of an innocent person, only one who was in league with him. Many claimed that a "specter" of a certain individual molested them, and because of the admittance of such evidence to the court of Oyer and Terminer, many were found guilty of witchcraft. Starkey succinctly states the consequences of such evidence:

> This was, as many good men and women were to discover, the sort of "proof" against which there is no disproof. Let an accuser say,

THE TRIAL SYSTEM OF THE SALEM WITCH TRIALS

"your shape came to my room last midnight," and the accused has no defense at all; no conceivable alibi can be furnished for the whereabouts of a "shape," one's airy substance.[25]

Once an individual was charged with molesting another by his "specter," there was virtually nothing he or she could do to prove the accusation false.

The point of issue was this: alleged victims claimed they were attacked by spirits in the likeness of some resident whom they identified. Was the evidence of mere allegation sufficient to convict the accused? If it was, who could escape hanging once the accusation was made?[26]

How can one explain why so many saw specters? Were the children deliberately accusing others falsely? Perhaps there is no satisfactory answer to this question. However, Smith may be correct when he states: "Their visions could have been very real, the product of hysteria induced by intense fear and excitement."[27] While one cannot rule out entirely the supernatural, the evidence seemingly points to the conclusion that many such instances were delusions. This could have been created by the intense peer pressure under which the young witnesses testified during the witch trials.

Throughout the trials Increase Mather acted cautiously as he wished for no innocent individual to be punished. Many times he argued the court's methods, especially spectral evidence, were unreliable.[28] Cotton Mather apparently also had from the beginning of the trials misgivings concerning the validity of spectral evidence.

> For my own part, I was alwayes afraid of proceeding to convict
> and condemn any person as a confederate with afflicting
> Daemons, upon so feeble an Evidence as a spectral Representation.
> Accordingly, I ever testified against it, both publickly and privately;
> and in my letters to the judges.[29]

There became, then, a gradual distrust of spectral evidence. In January 1693, the court of Oyer and Terminer was exchanged for a superior court. Spectral evidence was no longer considered valid, and only three of the fifty charged with witchcraft were indicted, but none of them were executed.[30] In May of the same year, Sir William issued a proclamation which released all who were charged with witchcraft; this act brought an end to the trials. Samuel Parris, whom many considered responsible for the entire episode, was required to leave Salem.

Results of the Trials

The aftermath of the violent witchcraft storm found many of the participants in a mournful and anguished state of mind. Many realized the complete folly of their accusations and delusions. The twelve jury members wrote in 1696:

> We confess that we our selves were not capable to understand nor
> able to withstand the mysterious delusions of the powers of dark-

ness and the Prince of the air.... We do heartily ask forgiveness of you all whom we have justly forgiven......We would none of us do such a thing again on such ground for the whole world.[31]

The climax of the "spirit of error" was in 1697 when the state of Massachusetts claimed a day of fasting for repentance of the innocent blood that was shed just five years earlier. Judge Samuel Sewall in public admitted his own guilt and asked forgiveness from God and humanity. In his diary he wrote:

> Samuel Sewall, sensible of the reiterated strokes of God upon himself and family and being sensible, that as to the Guilt contracted upon the opening of the late commission of Oyer and Terminer at Salem .... Desires to take the Blame and shame of it, Asking pardon of men, and especially desiring prayers that God... would pardon that sin and all other his sins.[32]

Ann Putnam, a major witness, made a similar confession in 1706. For years an atmosphere of remorse and guilt pervaded Salem for conducting the trials and other proceedings in such a hasty manner. Not only were the effects upon Salem psychological and social, but it also had important religious and political ramifications. The role that the leaders played in the Salem Witch Trials damaged their prestige and shook the foundation of unconstructed Puritanism.

THE CRY AT SALEM: AMERICA'S WITCHCRAFT TRIALS

Conclusion

There has been an attempt to demonstrate that the Salem Witch Trials were an outgrowth of the turbulent conditions prevalent in Salem during the 1680s and 1690s. No one factor can account for this unfortunate event in American history. It has been seen that among some of the causes were deep social and psychological conflicts prevalent within the community of Salem Village.

It has been displayed that these two causes, the social and the psychological, were two reasons for the outbreak of fear of witchcraft among the people of Salem. This book is not stating there was not witchcraft actually being practiced, whether it was voodoo, black magic, or white magic. There is historical evidence that such was occurring. However, there were other factors which were more dominant.

It is obvious why there was fear of witches. The Puritans believed themselves to be God's covenant people, and they expected demonic problems. The Indians and the constant fear of them reinforced in their thinking that their domain was being threatened. The religious and political problems seemingly were secondary, but they definitely added to the spirit of fear. The emerging secular spirit within Puritanism brought about sermons of a condemning nature; thus, there was a vacuum in the

Puritan soul. The colony also found itself in a turbulent state politically, and this added a spirit of uncertainty and confusion. Along with collective and individual psychological problems was the great social upheaval among Salem's citizens. Many were notorious for their gossiping and inability to accept one another. There also seemingly was a lack of constructive outlets for many of the children; thus, they naturally clashed with many of the older women.

After understanding the tremendous peer pressure under which the girls testified and accused others of witchcraft, one can understand why the children testified as they did. They were considered privileged citizens after making such accusations. After the trials, many of the witnesses admitted they had unjustly charged individuals of witchcraft; Ann Putnam, perhaps the major witness, made her confession in 1706.

This work is not an attempt to view the Salem Witch Trials in a rationalistic manner and de-emphasize the spiritual. There were recorded instances of witchcraft, but they seemingly were peripheral when compared to the vast social and psychological influences. These two forces dominated the lives of the people of Salem and led to one of the most tragic events in American history.

THE CRY AT SALEM: AMERICA'S WITCHCRAFT TRIALS

NOTES ON CHAPTERS

INTRODUCTION

1. David S. Schaff, *The Middle Ages*, vol. 6 of *History of the Christian Church*, by Philip Schaff, 8 vols. (New York Charles Scribner's Sons, 1910; reprint ed. Grand Rapids: Wm. B. Eerdmans Publishing Company, 1970), p. 515.

2. Ibid., p. 529

3. *Colliers Encyclopedia*, 1976 ed., s.v. "Witchcraft," by Marion L. Starkey, 23 552.

4. *Encyclopedia Americana*, 1964 ed., s.v. "Witchcraft," by Elizabeth E. Bacon, 29:84.

5. Donald Nugent, "The Renaissance and/or Witchcraft," *Church History* 40 (March 1971): 71.

6. James Warren, "On the Origins of Witchcraft in Christian Europe," *Trinity Journal* 5 (Spring 1976): 2.

7. Stuart Clark and P.T.J. Morgan, "Religion and Magic in Elizabethan Wales: Robert Holland's Dialog on Witchcraft," *Journal of Ecclesiastical History* 27 (January 1976): 33.

8. Peggy Robbins, "The Devil in Salem," *American History* 6 (December 1971) 6.

9. John Fisk, *The Beginnings of New England* (Boston: The Riverside Press, 1889), p. 243.

10. Samuel G. Darke, gen. ed., *The Witchcraft Delusion in New England: Its Rise, Progress, and Termination*, 3 vols. (n.p., 1866; reprint ed., New York: Burt Franklin, 1970), vol 1: *The Wonders of the Invisible World*, by Cotton Mather, pp. 15-17.

11. Linda R. Caporael, "Ergotism: The Satan Loosed in Salem?" *Science* 192 (April 1976): 23.

12. Frederick Drake, "Witchcraft in the American Colonies, 1647-62," *American Quarterly* 20 (Winter 1968): 697.

Chapter 1

1. Oliver Perry Chitwood, *A History of Colonial America*, 3rd ed. (New York: Harper & Brothers, 1921), p.102.

2. Perry Miller and Thomas H. Johnson, *The Puritans*, 2 vols. (New York: Harper and Row, 1963), 1: 149.

NOTES ON CHAPTERS

3. Perry Miller,"The Marrow of Puritan Divinity," in *The New England Puritans*, ed., Sydney V. James (New York: Harper and Row, 1968), p.13.

4. Ibid., p.20.

5. Richard A. Halser, "Our Puritan Heritage," *Christianity Today*, February 26, 1971, p. 23.

6. Thomas J. Wertenbaker, *The Puritan Oligarchy* (New York Charles Scribner's Sons, 1947) p. 59.

7. Greg L Bahnse, "Introduction to John Cotton's *Abstract of the Laws of New England*," *Journal of Christian Reconstruction* 2 (Winter 1975-76): 10.

8. James G. Blight, "Solomon Stoddard's *Safety of Appearing* and the Dissolution of the Puritan Faculty of Psychology," *Journal of the History of Behavioural Sciences* 10 (April 1974): 239.

9. Conrad Cherry, "New England as a Symbol: Ambiguity in the Puritan Vision," *Soundings* 58 (Fall 1975) 350.

10. Norman S. Fiering, "Will and Intellect in the New England Mind," *William and Mary Quarterly* 29 (October 1972) 551.

11. Stephen Foster, *Their Solitary Way* (New Haven: Yale University Press, 1971), p. 126.

12. T. McGiffert, ed., 2 vols., *Puritanism and the American Experience* (Reading: Wesley Publishing Co., 1969), 1 83.

13. Emory Elliot, *Power and the Pulpit in Puritan New England* (Princeton: Princeton University Press, 1975), p. 199.

14. Ralph Boas and Louise Boas, *Cotton Mather: Keeper of the Puritan Conscience* (New York: Harper and Brothers, 1928), p.91.

15. George M Stephenson, *The Puritan Heritage* (New York: The Macmillan Company, 1952), p. 32.

16. Ibid., p. 37.

17. William Haller, *The Puritan Frontier* (New York: AMS Press, 1968), p.45.

18. George F. Willison, *Saints and Strangers* (New York; Time Inc., 1914), p. 45.

19. Daniel J Boorstin, "The Anglicans," in *The Colonial Experience: Readings in Early American History*, ed., H. Trevor Colburn (Boston: Houghton Mifflin Company, 1966), p. 74.

20. Baird Tipson, "Invisible Saints: The 'Judgment of Charity' in the Early New England Churches," *Church History* 44 (December 1975):462.

21. James Thomas Meigs, "The Half-Way Covenant: A Study in Religious

Transition," *Foundations* 13 (April-June 1970):155-56.

22. Kai T. Erikson, *Wayward Puritans* (New York: John Wiley and Sons, Inc. 1966), p. 137.

23. Richard H. Werking, " 'Reformation Is Our Only Preservation,': Cotton Mather and Salem Witchcraft." *William and Mary Quarterly* 29 (April 1972):283.

24. Rosemary Katherine Twomey, "From Pure Church to Pure Nation: Massachusetts Bay, 1630-1692" (Ph.D. dissertation, University of Rochester, 1971), p. 222.

25. Sandford Fleming, *Children and Puritanism* (New Haven: Yale University Press, 1933) p. 73.

26. Ezra Byington, *The Puritan as Colonist and Reformer* (Boston: Little, Brown and Company, 1899), p. 177.

27. John F. Sena, "Melancholic Madness and the Puritans," *Harvard Theological Review* 66 (July 1973) 293-94.

28. Sally S. Booth, *The Witches of Early America* (New York: Hastings House Publishers, 1975), p. 202.

29. Marta Whitlock, "Voluntary Associations in Salem" (Ph.D. dissertation, Ohio State University, 1972), p. 242.

30. John Fisk, *New France and New England* (Boston: The Riverside

Press, 1902), p. 159.

31. Marion Starky, *The Devil in Massachusetts* (New York: Doubleday and Company, Inc., 1969), p. 23.

32. John R. Betts, "Mind and Body in Early American Thought," *Journal of American History* 54 (March 1968): 788.

33. Chadwick Hansen, "The Metamorphosis of Tituba," *New England Quarterly* 47 (March 1974): 4.

34. Daniel Howe, *The Puritan Republic* (Indianapolis: Bowen-Merrill Company, 1899), pp. 15-16.

35. James T Adams, *The Founding of New England* (Boston: The Atlantic Monthly Press, 1921), p. 394.

36. Kenneth B. Murdock, *Selections from Cotton Mather* (New York: Hafner Publishing Company, 1926), p. 394.

37. Roger Antonio Fortin, "The Decline of Royal Authority in Colonial Massachusetts" (Ph. D. dissertation, Lehigh University, 1969), p. 17.

38. T. H. Breen, *The Character of the Good Ruler* (New Haven: Yale University Press, 1970), p. 195.

39. Clarence L. Ver Steeg, *The Formative Years* 1697-1763 (New York: Hill and Wang, 1963), p. 146.

NOTES ON CHAPTERS

40. L. Lamprey, "Enduring Errors", *The American Mercury, Inc.* (January 1944) 46.

41. Erickson, *Wayward Puritans*, p. 155.

42. John C. Miller, *The Colonial Image* (New York: George Braziller Company, 1969), p. 185.

43. F. Schonemann, "Der Puritanismus in Neuengland", *Englische Studien* 59 (1925) 182.

44. Elliott, *Power and the Pulpit in Puritan New England*, p. 199.

45. Peter N. Carroll, *Puritanism and the Wilderness* (New York: Columbia University Press, 1969), p. 76-77.

46. Rossell Hope Robbins, "The Heresy of Witchcraft", *The South Atlantic Quarterly* 65 (Autumn 1966) 553.

47. Howe, *The Puritan Republic*, p. 93.

48. Starkey, *The Devil in Massachusetts*, p. 27.

49. Reuben G. Thwaites, *The Colonies* 1492-1750 (London: Longmans, Green and Company, 1922), p. 191.

50. Carl Holliday, *Woman's Life in Colonial Days* (New York: Frederick Ungar Publishing Company, 1922), p. 55.

51. Paul Boyer and Stephen Nissenbaum, *Salem Possessed* (Cambridge: Harvard University Press, 1974). P. 103.

52. Erickson, *Wayward Puritans,* p. 139.

53. Fleming, *Children and Puritanism,* p. 153.

54. Lazer Ziff, *Puritanism in America* (New York: The Viking Press, 1973), p. 147.

CHAPTER II

1. Cotton Mather and Increase Mather, *The Wonders of the Invisible World* (London: John Russell Smith, 1862), pp. 225-253.

2. Paul Boyer and Stephen Nissenbaum, *Salem Possessed* (Cambridge: Harvard University Press, 1974), p. 3.

3. James D. Phillips, *Salem in the Seventeenth Century* (Boston: Houghton and Mifflin Company, 1933), pp. 290-308.

4. *Records of Salem Witchcraft Copied from the Original Documents,* 2 vols. (Roxbury, Massachusetts: W. Elliot Woodard, 1863; reprint ed., New York: Da Capo Press, 1969), 1:44-45.

5. Ibid., 1:13-32.

6. Ibid., 1:39-40.

NOTES ON CHAPTERS

7. Ibid., 1:40-41.

8. Ibid., 1:75

9. Ibid., 1:90-91.

10. Sally Booth, *The Witches of Early America* (New York: Hastings House Publishers, 1975) p. 207.

11. Samuel G. Drake, ed., *Annals of Witchcraft in New England* (n.p., 1869; reprint ed., New york: Burt Franklin, 1972), p. 189.

12. *Dictionary of American History*, 1976 ed., s.v. "Witchcraft", by James Duncan Phillips.

13. James William Clark, Jr., "The Tradition of Salem Witchcraft in American Literature 1820-1870" (Ph.D. dissertation, Duke University, 1970), p. 17.

14. Marion Starky, *The Devil in Massachusetts,* (New York: Doubleday and Company, Inc., 1969), p. 68.

15. Peggy Robbins, "The Devil in Salem", *American History* 6 (December 1971):44.

16. Dennis E. Owen, "Satan's Fiery Darts:Explorations into the Experience and Concept of the Demonic in the Seventeenth Century New England" (Ph. D. dissertation, Princeton University, 1974), p. 289.

17. Charles V. Upham, *Salem Witchcraft*, 2 vols. (New York: Frederick Ungar Publishing Company, n.d.), 2:12-13.

18. *Records of Salem Witchcraft Copied from the Original Documents,* 1:17-19.

19. Samuel Drake, gen. ed., *The Witchcraft Delusion in New England: Its Rise, Progress and Termination,* 3 vols. (n.p., 1866; reprint ed., New York: Burt Franklin, 1970), vol. 3: *More Wonders of the invisible World,* by Robert Calef, p. 34.

20. Owen, "Satan's Fiery Darts", p.293.

21. Winfield S. Nevins, *Witchcraft in Salem Village in 1692* (New York: Burt Franklin, 1971), p. 66.

22. *Records of Salem Witchcraft Copied from the Original Documents,* 1:36-37.

23. Upham, *Salem Witchcraft,* 2:88-89.

24. Nevins, *Witchcraft in Salem Village in 1692,* pp. 111-16.

25. Chadwick Hansen, *Witchcraft at Salem* (New York: George Braziller Company, 1969), p. 51.

26. *Records of Salem Witchcraft Copied from the Original Documents,* 1:82.

Notes on Chapters

27. Ibid., 1:82, 83, 85.

28. Nevins, *Witchcraft in Salem Village in 1692*, pp. 190-91.

29. Ibid., pp. 190-91.

30. Samuel Drake, gen. Ed., *The Witchcraft Delusion in New England: Its Rise, Progress and Termination*, 3 vols. (n.p., 1866; reprint ed., New York: Burt Franklin, 1970), vol. *1: The Wonders of the Invisible World*, by Cotton Mather, p. 178.

31. *Records of Salem Witchcraft Copied from the Original Documents*, 1:200-03.

32. Hansen, *Witchcraft at Salem*, p. 151.

33. *Records of Salem Witchcraft Copied from the Original Documents*, 2:31-32.

34. Ibid., 2:32-33

35. George Lincoln Burr, ed., *Narratives of the Witchcraft Cases* (n.p., 1914; reprint ed., New York: Barnes and Noble Inc., 1959), pp. 368-69.

36. Sarah Comstock, "A Broomstick Journey to Old Salem", *The World Review* 7 (October 29, 1928) 111.

37. Mark Van Doren, ed., *Samuel Sewall's Diary* (New York: Russell and Russell, 1963), p. 108.

38. Starky, *The Devil in Massachusetts*, p. 68.

39. Hansen, *Witchcraft at Salem*, p. 86.

40. Booth, *The Witches of Early America*, p. 207.

41. "Clark, The Tradition of Salem Witchcraft in American Literature 1820-1870", p. 17.

42. Emil Oberholzer, Jr., "Saints in Sin: A Study of the Disciplinary Action of the Congregational Churches in Massachusetts in the Colonial and Early National Periods" (Ph. D. Dissertation, Columbia University, 1954), p. 113.

43. Upham, *Salem Witchcraft*, 2:394-95.

CHAPTER III

1. John Demos, "Underlying Themes in the witchcraft of Seventeenth Century New England", *American Historical Review* 75 (June 1970):1317.

2. Ibid., p. 1315.

3. Ibid., p. 1316.

4. Marion Starky, *The Devil in Massachusetts* (New York: Doubleday and

NOTES ON CHAPTERS

Company, Inc. 1969), pp. 49, 53.

5. Louis B. Wright, *The Atlantic Frontier* (New York: Alfred A. Knopf Company, 1947), p. 157.

6. Starky, *The Devil in Massachusetts*, p. 101.

7. George Lincoln Burr, ed., *Narratives of the Witchcraft Cases* (n.p., 1914; reprint ed., New York: Barnes and Noble, Inc., 1959), p. 356.

8. Samuel G. Drake, ed., *Annals of Witchcraft in New England* (n.p., 1869; reprint ed., New York: Burt Franklin, 1972), p. 197.

9. Chadwick Hansen, *Witchcraft at Salem* (New York: George Braziller Company, 1969), p. 76.

10. Charles V. Upham, *Salem Witchcraft*, 2 vols. (New York: Frederick Ungar Publishing Company, n.d.), 2:300-01

11. Paul Boyer and Stephen Nissenbaum, *Salem Possessed* (Cambridge: Harvard University Press, 1974), p. 146.

12. Katherine Bryn, "The Sins of Salem", *Science Digest* 69 (May 1971):30.

13. Hansen, *Witchcraft at Salem*, p. 71.

14. Stephen Foster, *Their Solitary Way* (New Haven: Yale University Press, 1971), p. 28.

15. James W Jones, *The Shattered Synthesis* (New Haven: Yale University Press, 1973) p. 104.

16. Samuel G. Drake, ed., *Annals of Witchcraft in New England,* p. 191.

17. Kai T Erickson, *Wayward Puritans* (New York: John Wiley and Sons, Inc., 1966), p. 149.

18. Thomas J Wertenbaker, *The Puritan Oligarchy* (New York: Charles Scribner's Sons, 1947), pp. 278-79.

19. John Demos, "Underlying Themes in New England Witchcraft", in *Puritanism in Early America,* ed., George M. Waller, 2nd ed., (Lexington, Massachusetts: D.C. Heath and Company, 1973), p.184.

CHAPTER IV

1. Joseph Botond-Blazek, "Puritans and Sex: An Inquiry into the Legal Enforcement of Sexual Morality in 17th Century Massachusetts", Ph.D. dissertation, University of California, 1962), p.99.

2. Marion Starkey, *The Devil in Massachusetts* (New York: Doubleday and Company, Inc., 1969), p. 153.

3. Daniel Howe, *The Puritan Republic* (Indianapolis: Bowen-Merrill Company, 1899),
P. 71.

NOTES ON CHAPTERS

4. Ralph Boas and Louise Boas, *Cotton Mather: Keeper of the Puritan Conscience* (New York: Harper and Brothers, 1928), p. 109.

5. Cotton Mather, *Boniface: An Essay to Do Good* (Gainsville:Scholar's Facsimiles and reprints, 1976), p.153.

6. Emil Oberholzer, Jr., "Saints in Sin: A Study of the Disciplinary Action of the Congregational Churches in Massachusetts in the Colonial and Early National Periods" (Ph. D. dissertation, Columbia University, 1954), p. 115.

7. Winfield S. Nevins, *Witchcraft in Salem Village in 1692* (New York: Burt Franklin, 1971), p. 92-93.

8. Emory Elliot, *Power and the Pulpit in Puritan New England* (Princeton: Princeton University Press, 1975), p. 200.

9. Cotton Mather, *The Wonders of the Invisible World,* quoted in George L. Burr, ed., *Narratives of the Witch Cases* (New York: Barnes and Nobel, Inc., 1914), p. 246.

10. Kenneth B. Murdock, *Increase Mather* (Cambridge: Harvard University Press, 1926), p. 293.

11. Abijah Marvin, *The Life and Times of Cotton Mather* (Boston: Congregational Sunday School and Publishing Society, 1892), p. 139.

12. Samuel Mather, *The Life of Cotton Mather* (New York: Garrett Press,

Inc., 1970), p. 45.

13. Lazer Ziff, *Puritanism in America* (New York: The Viking Press, 1973), p. 243.

14. N.H. Chamberlain, *Samuel Sewall and the World He Lived In* (Boston: De Wolfe, Fisk and Company, 1897), p. 168.

15. Robert Middlekauft, *The Mathers: Three Generations of Puritan Intellectuals* (New York: Oxford University Press, 1971), p. 156.

16. Chadwick Hansen, *Witchcraft at Salem* (New York: George Braxiller Company,
1969), p. 98.

17. John Oldmixon, *The British Empire in America* (New York; August M. Kelly, 1969), p. 190.

18. Starkey, *The Devil in Massachusetts,* p. 51.

19. Sally S. Booth, *The Witches of Early America* (New York: Hastings House Publishers, 1975), p. 210.

20. Ezra Byington, *The Puritan as Colonist and Reformer* (Boston: Little, Brown and Company, 1899), p. 178.

21. Kai T. Erikson, *Wayward Puritans* (New York: John Wiley and Sons, Inc., 1966), p. 151.

NOTES ON CHAPTERS

22. Samuel G. Drake, ed., *Annals of Witchcraft in New England* (n.p., 1869; reprint ed., New York: Burt Franklin, 1972), p. 189.

23. Robert Smith, *The Massachusetts Colony* (London: Collier-Macmillan, Ltd., 1969), p. 40.

24. Paul Boyer and Stephen Nissenbaum, *Salem Possessed* (Cambridge: Harvard University press, 1974), p. 215.

25. Starkey, *The Devil in Massachusetts*, p. 37.

26. Perry Miller and Thomas Johnson, *The Puritans*, 2 vols. (New York: Harper and Row, 1963), 2:736.

27. Smith, *The Massachusetts Colony*, p. 44.

28. Robert Middlekauft, *The Mathers: Three Generations of Puritan Intellectuals*, p. 154.

29. Cotton Mather, *The Diary of Cotton Mather*, 2 vols. (New York: Frederick Ungar Publishing Company, 1957), 1:150.

30. Barrett Wendell, *Cotton Mather, The Puritan Priest* (New York: Harcourt, Brace and World, Inc., 1891), p. 73.

31. Robert Calef, *More Wonders of the Invisible World*, quoted in Burr, *Narratives of the Witchcraft Cases*, pp. 387-88.

32. Mark Van Doren, ed., *Samuel Sewall's Diary* (New York: Russell and Russell, 1963), p. 139.

THE CRY AT SALEM: AMERICA'S WITCHCRAFT TRIALS

SELECTED BIBLIOGRAPHY

BOOKS

Adams, Charles F. *Three Episodes of Massachusetts History.* 3 vols. New York: Russell and Russell, 1892.

Adams, James T. *The Founding of New England.* Boston: The Atlantic Monthly Press, 1921.

Beard, George M. *The Psychology of the Salem Witchcraft Excitement of 1692.* New York: G. P. Putnam's Sons, 1882.

Bell, Hesketh J. *Obeah: Witchcraft in the West Indies.* Westport: Negro University Press, 1970.

Boas, Ralph and Boas, Louise. *Cotton Mather: Keeper of the Puritan Conscience.* New York: Harper and Brothers, 1928.

Bonfanti, Leo. *The Witchcraft Hysteria of 1692.* Wakefield: Pride Publications, Inc., 1971.

Boorstin, Daniel J. "The Anglicans." In *The Colonial Experience: Reading*

THE CRY AT SALEM: AMERICA'S WITCHCRAFT TRIALS

in *Early American History,* pp. 73-79. Edited by H.Trevor Colbourn. Boston: Houghton Mifflin Company, 1966.

Booth, Sally S. *The Witches of Early America.* New York: Hastings House Publishers, 1975.

Boyer, Paul and Nissenbaum, Stephen. *Salem Possessed.* Cambridge: Harvard University Press, 1974.

Breen, T. H. *The Character of the Good Ruler.* New Haven: Yale University Press, 1970.

Burr, George Lincoln, ed. *Narratives of the Witchcraft Cases.* N.p., 1914 reprint ed., New York: Barnes & Noble, Inc., 1959.

Byington, Ezra. *The Puritan as Colonist and Reformer.* Boston: Little, Brown and Company, 1899.

Carroll, Peter N. *Puritanism and the Wilderness.* New York: Columbia University Press, 1969.

Chamberlain, N. H. *Samuel Sewall and the World He Lived In.* Boston: De Wolfe, Fish and Company, 1897.

Chamberlain, Samuel. *A Stroll through Historic Salem.* New York: Hastings House Publishers, 1969.

Chitwood, Oliver Perry. *A History of Colonial America.* 3rd ed. New York: Harper & Brothers, 1931.

SELECTED BIBLIOGRAPHY

Craven, Wesley Frank. *The Colonies in Transition: 1660-1713*. New York: Harper and Row Publishers, 1968.

Demos, John. *Remarkable Providences 1600-1760*. New York: George Braziller, 1972.

Drake, Samuel G., ed. *Annals of Witchcraft in New England*. N.p., 1869; reprint ed., New York: Burt Franklin, 1972.

Drake, Samuel G., gen. ed., *The Witchcraft Delusion in New England: Its Rise, Progress, and Termination*. 3 vols. N.p. 1866; reprint ed., New York: Burt Franklin, 1970. Vol. 1: *The Wonders of the Invisible World*, by Cotton Mather. Vol. 3: *More Wonders of the Invisible World*, by Robert Calef.

Elliott, Emory. *Power and the Pulpit in Puritan New England*. Princeton: Princeton University Press, 1975.

Ellis, George E. *The Puritan Age and Rule in Massachusetts*. Boston: Mifflin and Company, 1888.

Erikson, Kai T. *Wayward Puritans*. New York: John Wiley and Sons, Inc., 1966.

Fisk, John. *The Beginnings of New England*. Boston: The Riverside Press, 1889.

_____. *New France and New England*. Boston: The RIverside Press, 1902.

Fleming, Sandford. *Children and Puritanism.* New Haven:Yale University Press, 1933.

Foster, Stephen. *Their Solitary Way.* New Haven:Yale University Press, 1971.

Gaer, Joseph, and Siegel, Ben. *The Puritan Heritage.* New York:The New American Library, 1964.

Gemmill, William N. *The Salem Witch Trials.* Chicago:A. C. McClurg and Company, 1924.

Haller, William. *The Puritan Frontier.* New York:AMS Press, 1968.

Hansen, Chadwick. *Witchcraft at Salem.* New York: George Braziller Company, 1969.

Holliday, Carl. *Woman's Life in Colonial Days.* New York: Frederick Ungar Publishing Company, 1922.

Hosmer, James K., ed. *Winthrop's Journal.* 2 vols. New York: Barnes and Noble, Inc., 1908.

Howe, Daniel. *The Puritan Republic,* Indianapolis: Bowen-Merrill Company, 1899.

James, Sydney V., ed. *The New England Puritans.* New York: Harper and Row, 1968.

Selected Bibliography

Jones, James W. The *Shattered Synthesis.* New Haven: Yale University Press, 1973.

Kittredge, George L. *Witchcraft in Old and New England.* New York: Russell and Russell, 1929.

Lawrence, Henry W. *The Not-Quite Puritans.* Boston: Little, Brown and Company, 1928.

Levin, David. *What Happened in Salem?* New York: Harcourt, Brace and World, Inc., 1960.

Marvin, Abijah. *The Life and Times of Cotton Mather.* Boston: Congregational Sunday School and Publishing Society, 1892.

Mather, Cotton. *Boniface: An Essay to Do Good.* Gainsville: Scholar's Facsimiles and Reprints, 1967.

_____. *The Diary of Cotton Mather.* 2 vols. New York: Frederick Ungar Publishing Company, 1957.

Mather, Cotton, and Mather, Increase. *The Wonders of the Invisible World.* London: John Russell Smith, 1862.

Mather, Samuel. *The Life of Cotton Mather.* Boston: By the Author for Samuel Gerish 1729; reprint ed., New York: Garrett Press, Inc., 1970.

McGiffert, T., ed. *Puritanism and the American Experience.* 2 vols.

Reading: Wesley Publishing Company, 1969.

Middlekauft, Robert. *The Mathers: Three Generations of Puritan Intellectuals.* New York: Oxford University Press, 1971.

Miller, John C. *The Colonial Image.* New York: George Braziller Company, 1969.

Miller, Perry. "The Marrow of Puritan Divinity." In *The New England Puritans,* pp. 12-42. Edited by Sydney V. James. New York: Harper and Row, 1968.

Miller, Perry and Johnson, Thomas H. *The Puritans.* 2 vols. New York: Harper ad Row, 1963.

Monter, William E. *European Witchcraft.* New York: John Wiley and Sons, 1969.

Murdock, Kenneth B. *Increase Mather.* Cambridge: Harvard University Press, 1926.

_____. *Selections from Cotton Mather.* New York: Hafner Publishing Company, 1926.

Nevins, Winfield S. *Witchcraft in Salem Village in 1692.* New York: Burt Franklin, 1971.

Oldmixon, John. *The British Empire in America.* New York: August M. Kelley, 1969.

SELECTED BIBLIOGRAPHY

Phillips, James D. *Salem in the Seventeenth Century.* Boston: Houghton and Mifflin Company, 1933.

Records of Salem Witchcraft Copied from the Original Documents. 2 vols. Roxbury, Massachusetts: W. Elliott Woodward, 1864; reprint ed., New York: Da Capo Press, 1969.

Russell, Jeffrey B. *Witchcraft in the Middle Ages.* Ithaca: Cornell University Press, 1972.

Rutman, Darrett. *Winthrop's Boston.* Chapel Hill: University of North Carolina Press, 1965.

Schaff, Davis . *The Middle Ages.* Vol. 6 of *History of the Christian Church,* by Phillip Schaff. 8 vols. New York: Charles Scribner's Sons, 1910; reprint ed., Grand Rapids: Wm. B. Eerdmans Publishing Company, 1970.

Schlesinger, Arthur M., and Fox, Dixon R., gen. eds. *A History of American Life.* 12 vols. New York: The MacMillan Company 1927. Vol. 2: *The First Americans 1607-90,* by Thomas Jefferson Wertenbaker.

Smith, Robert. *The Massachusetts Colony.* London: Collier-Macmillan, Ltd. 1969.

Starkey, Marion. *The Devil in Massachusetts.* New York: Doubleday and Company, Inc., 1969.

_____. *The Visionary Girls,* Witchcraft in Salem Village. Boston: Little Brown and Company, 1973.

Stephenson, George M. *The Puritan Heritage.* New York: The Macmillan Company, 1952.

Sweet, William. *The Story of Religion in America.* Grand Rapids: Baker Book House, 1973.

Thwaites, Reuben G. *The Colonies 1492-1750.* London: Longmans, Green and Company, 1913.

Upham, Charles V. *Salem Witchcraft.* 2 vols. New York: Russell and Russell, 1963.

Van Doren, Mark, ed. *Samuel Sewell's Diary.* New York: Russell and Russell, 1963.

Ver Steeg, Clarence L. *The Formative Years, 1607-1763.* New York: Hill and Wang, 1964.

Waller, George M., ed. *Puritanism in Early America.* Lexington, Massachusetts: D.C. Heath and Company, 1973.

Wendell, Barrett. *Cotton Mather: The Puritan Priest.* New York: Harcourt, Brace and World, Inc., 1891.

Wertenbaker, Thomas J. *The Puritan Oligarchy.* New York: Charles Scribner's Sos, 1947.

SELECTED BIBLIOGRAPHY

Wickwar, J.W. *Witchcraft and the Black Art.* London: Herbert Jenkins, Ltd., n.d.

Willison, George F. *Saints and Strangers.* New York: Time, Inc., 1914.

Winwar, Francis, *Puritan City.* New York: National Travel Club, 1938.

Wright. Louis B. *The Atlantic Frontier* .New York: Alfred A. Knopf Company, 1947.

Ziff, Larzer. *Puritanism in America.* New York: The Viking Press, 1973.

DICTIONARIES AND ENCYCLOPEDIAS

Colliers Encyclopedia, 1976 ed. S. v. "Witchcraft," by Marion L. Starkey.

Dictionary of American History, 1976 ed. S. v. "Witchcraft," by James Duncan Phillips.

Encyclopedia Americana, 1964 ed. S. v. "Witchcraft," by Elizabeth E. Bacon

The New Catholic Encyclopedia, 1967 ed. S. v. "Witchcraft," by F. Merzbacher.

The New Schaff-Herzog Encyclopedia of Religious Knowledge, 1912 ed. S. v. "Witchcraft," by George Gilmore.

DISSERTATIONS

Bloom, Jeanne Gould. "Sir Edmond Andros: A Study in Seventeenth Century Colonial Administration." Ph.D. dissertation, Yale University, 1962.

Botand-Blazek, Joseph. "Puritans and Sex. An Inquiry into the Legal Enforcement of Sexual Morality in 17th Century Massachusetts." Ph.D. dissertation, University of California, 1962.

Clark, James William, Jr. "The Tradition of Salem Witchcraft in American Literature 1820-1870." Ph.D. dissertation, Duke University, 1970.

Cross, Arthur Lyon. "The Anglican Episcopate and the American Colonies." Ph.D. dissertation, Harvard University, 1899.

Cunningham, Homer, "The Effect of the Decline of the Puritan Oligarchy upon the Schools of Massachusetts between 1664 and 1758." Ph.D. dissertation, New York University, 1954.

Fortin, Roger Antonio. "The Decline of Royal Authority in Colonial Massachusetts." Ph.D. dissertation, Lehigh University, 1969.

Gildrie, Richard. "Salem, 1626-1668: History of a Covenant Community." Ph.D. dissertation, University of Virginia, 1971.

New, John Frederick Hamilton. "Anglican and Puritan: The Basis of Their

SELECTED BIBLIOGRAPHY

Opposition Reconsidered." Ph.D. dissertation, University of Toronto, 1963.

Notestein, Wallace. "A History of English Witchcraft from 1558-1718." Ph.D. dissertation, Yale University, 1908.

Oberholzer, Emil, Jr. "Saints in Sin: A Study of the Disciplinary Action of the Congregational Churches of Massachusetts in the Colonial and Early National Periods." Ph.D. dissertation, Columbia University, 1954.

Owen, Dennis E. "Satan's Fiery Darts: Explorations into the Experience and Concept of the Demonic in Seventeenth Century New England." Ph.D. dissertation, Princeton University, 1974.

Perluck, Herbert Allen. "Puritan Expression and the Decline of Piety." Ph.D. dissertation, Princeton University, 1974.

Shadel, Gerald Lee. "The Anglican Mind of the 1960s." Ph.D. dissertation, University of Maryland, 1963.

Twomey, Rosemary Katharine. "From Pure Church to Pure Nation: Massachusetts Bay, 1630-1692." Ph.D. dissertation, University of Rochester, 1971.

Whitlock, Marta. "Voluntary Associations in Salem, Massachusetts before 1800." Ph.D. dissertation, Ohio State University, 1972.

THE CRY AT SALEM: AMERICA'S WITCHCRAFT TRIALS

PERIODICALS

Bahnsen, Greg L. "Introduction to John Cotton's *Abstract of the Laws of New England.*" *Journal of Christian Reconstruction* 2 (Winter 1975-76):110-28.

Betts, John R. "Mind and Body in Early American Thought." *Journal of American History* 54 (March 1968):787-805.

Blight, James G. "Solomon Stoddard's Safety of Appearing and Dissolution of the Puritan Faculty of Psychology." *Journal of the History of Behavioral Sciences* 10 (April 1974):238-50.

Breen, Timothy. "Who Governs: The Town Franchise in Seventeenth Century Massachusetts." *William and Mary Quarterly* 27 (October 1970):460-74.

Bryn, Katherine. "The Sins of Salem." *Science Digest* 69 (May 1971):29-31.

Caporael, Linnda R. "Ergotism: The Satan Loosed in Salem?" *Science* 192 (April 1976):21-26.

Carey, George G. "Folklore from the Printed Sources of Essex County, Massachusetts." *Southern Folklore Quarterly* 32 (March 1968):17-43.

Cherry, Conrad. "New England as a Symbol: Ambiguity in the Puritan Vision." *Soundings* 58 (Fall 1975):348-60.

Clark, Stuart and Morgan, P.T.J. "Religion and Magic in Elizabethan Wales:

SELECTED BIBLIOGRAPHY

Robert Hollands' Dialogue on Witchcraft." *Journal of Ecclesiastical History* 27 (January 1976):31-46.

Cohen, Ronald. "Church and State in Seventeenth-Century Massachusetts: Another Look at the Antinomian Controversy." *Journal of Church and State* 12 (Winter 1970):475-94.

Comstock, Sarah. "A Broomstick Ride to Old Salem." *The World Review* 7 (October 29, 1928):103-110-11.

Connor, John. "The Social and Psychological Reality of European Witchcraft Beliefs." *Psychiatry* 38 (November 1975):366-80.

Deibler, Edwin C. "The Chief Characteristic of Early English Puritanism." B*ibliotheca Sacra* 129 (October-December 1972):326-35.

Demos, John, "Underlying Themes in the Witchcraft of Seventeenth Century New England." *American Historical Review* 75(June 1970):1311-26.

Drake, Frederick. "Witchcraft in the American Colonies, 1647-62." *American Quarterly* 20 (Winter 1968):694-725.

Feinstein, Howard M. "The Prepared Heart: A Comparative Study of Puritan Theology and Psychoanalysis." *American Quarterly* 22 (Spring 1970):166-766.

Feiring, Norman S. "Will and Intellect in the New England Mind." *William and Mary Quarterly* 29 (October 1972):515-58.

Hansen, Chadwick, "The Metamorphosis of Tituba." *New England Quarterly* 47(March 1974)3-12.

Hasler, Richard A. "Our Puritan Heritage." *Christianity Today* 15 (February 26, 1971):23-24.

Lamprey, L. "Enduring Errors." *The American Mercury, Inc.* 58 (January 1944):46-50.

Lazenby, Walter. "Exhortation as Exorcism: Cotton Mather's Sermons to Murderers." *Quarterly Journal of Speech* 57 (February 1971):50-56.

Meigs, James Thomas. "The Half-Way Covenant: A Study in Religious Transition." *Foundations* 12 (April-June 1970):142-58.

Nash, Dennison. "A Convergence of Psychological and Social Explanations of Witchcraft." *Current Anthropology* 14 (December 1973):545-46.

Nugent, Donald. "The Renaissance and/or Witchcraft." *Church History* 40 (March 1971):69-78.

Robbins, Peggy. "The Devil in Salem." *American History* 6 (December 1971):6-9, 44-48.

Robbins, Russell Hope. "The Heresy of Witchcraft." *The South Atlantic Quarterly* 65 (Autumn 1966):532-43.

Sana, John F. "Melancholic Madness and the Puritans." *Harvard*

SELECTED BIBLIOGRAPHY

Theological Review 66 (July 1973):293-309.

Schönemann, F. "Der Puritanismus in Neuengland." *Englische Studien* 58 (1925):173-92.

Simmons, Richard C. "Early Massachusetts." *History Today* 28 (April 1968):259-67.

Teall, John L. "Witchcraft and Calvinism in Elizabethan England: Divine Power and Human Agency. "*Journal of the History of Ideas* 23 (January-March 1962):21-36.

Tipson, Baird. "Invisible Saints: The 'Judgement of Charity' in the Early New England Churches." *Church History* 44 (December 1975):460-71.

Vartanian, Pershing. "Cotton Mather and the Puritan Translation into the Enlightenment." *Early American Literature* 7 (Winter 1973):213-24.

Warren, James. "On the Origins of Witchcraft in Christian Europe." *Trinity Journal* 5 (Spring 1976):1-20.

Werking, Richard H. " 'Reformation is Our Only Preservation': Cotton Mather ad Salem Witchcraft." *William and Mary Quarterly* 29 (April 1972):280-90.

THE CRY AT SALEM: AMERICA'S WITCHCRAFT TRIALS

About the Author

Jeffrey Jon Richards is a minister and theology professor who lives with his family in North Carolina. He received the Th.M. degree from Dallas Theological Seminary and the Ph.D. in systematic theology from Drew University. He has done postdoctoral work at Oxford (England), Marburg, and Tuebingen (Germany). He has taught on the faculties of several American and European universities and seminaries.

THE CRY AT SALEM: AMERICA'S WITCHCRAFT TRIALS

www.ingramcontent.com/pod-product-compliance
Lightning Source LLC
Chambersburg PA
CBHW070511090426
42735CB00012B/2729